The one and lonely Kidar Sharma

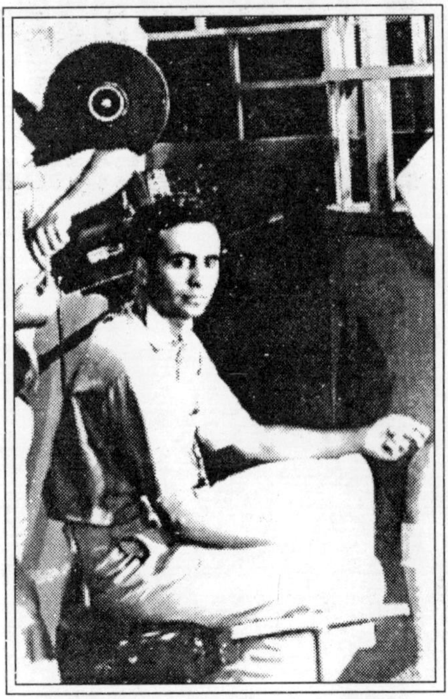

The one and lonely Kidar Sharma

[an anecdotal autobiography]

edited by

Dr. Vikram Sharma

BLUEJAY BOOKS

An imprint of Srishti Publishers & Distributors
New Delhi & Calcutta

BLUEJAY BOOKS
An imprint of SRISHTI PUBLISHERS & DISTRIBUTORS
64-A, Adhchini
Sri Aurobindo Marg
New Delhi 110 017
srishtipublishers@forindia.com

First published by
BLUEJAY BOOKS 2002

ISBN 81-87075-96-1
Rs. 250.00

Cover Design: Mark Johnston
Book design: Billy Sharma

Typeset in Goudy Old Style 12 at
45 Nehru Apartment, Kalkaji, New Delhi 110 019
arrt@vsnl.com

Printed and bound in India by
YUGEEN PRINTERS
B-52,sector 8,Noida-201301

Dedicated to my loving wife

Raj Dulari

who had to bear my severe poverty and struggle,

my dreams and disappointments,

and three wonderful children.

Introduction

My association with Mr. Kidar Sharma goes back, literally, to the day I was born. He was a neighbour of my parents, and it was in his car that my mother was taken to hospital, on the day she delivered me. Today, as I pen the introduction to his anecdotal biography, so many thoughts and memories crowd my mind.

What do I remember most about him? Perhaps it was his wry and, at times, self-deprecating humour. He could come up with a wise-crack, a joke, an ironic piece of poetry or a quotable quote, that aptly summed up a situation and embedded it in our memory. And then, there were his stories! He was a raconteur of tales and experiences, and there was something about the way he narrated them that always amazed me. Even though, so often, the stories were, inherently, chronicles of sadness and despair, what came across to me, as an adolescent and later as a young man, was a strangely funny and comical vision of the human condition. Later, years later, I came to realize that this was Mr. Sharma's method of soothing the wounds that he would otherwise find unbearable.

And how did Mr. Sharma get his wounds? He was a driven man. Nothing mattered more to him than cinema. Every aspect of its creation. For him the art of film-making meant the integration of several disciplines – painting, architecture, music, sound and image construction. And he partook passionately in all of them.

This obsession began early in his life. He was an avid cinema-goer, and one day he happened to see a film called *Puran Bhagat* directed by Mr. D.K. Bose. It changed his entire perception of cinema. Here was a film that freed the medium from its theatrical moorings. He was fascinated by its experiments with background music, its use of silences to evoke mood, its subtle use of images and composition to convey the story and its symbolism to underline ideas. Cinema was not just an image-recording device, but much, much more.

Mr. Kidar Sharma was hooked! He just had to go to Calcutta and apprentice with the director who had opened his eyes to the medium – Shri D. K. Bose. He was in his early twenties and, against the wishes of his parents, with money borrowed from his young bride, Mr. Sharma headed out of his little village of Narowal in the Punjab in search of his dream. This drive and conviction remained with him throughout his life.

He believed that cinema was the total vision of one individual – the director. So, he performed the scenes for his actors, wrote the lyrics for his songs, penned the dialogue, keenly participated in the composing of the music and directed the film. When there was no producer around to back his films, he produced them himself.

But the world of cinema was changing. By the mid-sixties, the discipline and the camaraderie of the studio productions was rapidly being replaced by the anarchy of the star system. Scripts sourced from classical literary works were giving way to other more contemporary themes. And most importantly, cinema was increasingly being seen only as a medium of entertainment, capable of raking in enormous profits. In fact profits became the overriding criteria for producing films – sometimes at the cost of everything else.

And yet Mr. Kidar Sharma traversed his own path. But in the prevailing scenario, he was making fewer films, and by the late seventies and eighties, fewer still. But he kept on.

I recall meeting him in 1987 (he would have been close to 80 years old) and asking him what he was doing at the time. "Oh" he said, chirpily "I'm shooting a new film!'. "How do you manage to do it?" I asked. "It's easy" he smiled and replied. "Whenever I get some money from the re-sale of my earlier films, I shoot a bit. See how my past is paying for my future!"

Mr. Kidar Sharma completed his last film in 1993. I'm absolutely sure he would have gone on, but his past had begun to dry up. How many times can you earn money from the re-sale rights of your earlier work?

For the man, who had participated in the making of *Devdas, Vidyapati, Chitralekha, Neel Kamal, Suhag Raat, Jogan, Bawre Nain, Hamari Yaad Aayegi* and so many more wonderful films, the journey was over.

Mr. Kidar Sharma died in 1999, dreaming till the last of the films he wanted to make. He always had a subject ready, or a script waiting to be financed. It never happened. And strange as it may seem, he was, I think, the only significant film-maker who was not adequately honoured in this country in his lifetime.

Saeed Akhtar Mirza
Mumbai

Prologue

This book has not been written by an angel, therefore all 'angels' are advised not to touch it. I have never been comfortable among them. I love human beings with all their faults, failures, weaknesses and silly, sinful escapades. After all, they are flesh and temptation together, whereas angels, I feel, are the sycophants of the divine deception, called GOD. Perhaps I have always been anti-authority or at least ambivalent, not so much consciously, although there are hints in my writings. "*Tumm javo javo bhagwan bane, insaan bano toe jaane*". (Go on, keep playing God, become a human to be really acknowledged.) Again... "*Betaab tayray jalvoon kay leiya, woh aaur koyee moosa hoga tayray jalve dhoonday gay jisse, woh mera dil-e-deewana hai.*" (Some other Moses may hanker for Your dazzling miracles, The crazy heart Your miracles will seek is mine.) And again... "*bandoon say durr durr mohabbat say be-niz, aisay khuds say meri nibhhaygee na aik din.*" (Aloof from humanity, unconcerned with love, with such a God, I cannot get along even for a day). These are some examples from my writings. Let me focus on my relationships with mortals, now.

Chapter 1

"The world was too young"

G. Garcia.

The twentieth century was barely a decade old, when I was sent to land on this planet, the good earth. It was a frightfully stormy night with heavy showers and howling winds; trees trembled, branches shivered and terrified tiny leaves tried to flee. In the dark sky, lightning danced her Tandav (Shiva's dance of destruction), accompanied by a thousand thundering drums.

In a small village in Punjab known as Narowal, inside a dark, dingy, dank room with mud walls, and one small window, my young mother was going through the pangs of childbirth. Some good-natured neighbouring woman had come to render help. My grandmother was too old. My father had left home in the morning to fetch the village Dayee and was not yet back. This dayee, the old fashioned village midwife, who attended to all the deliveries of this area, could not be traced that day. My father chased her from village to village, from hutment to hutment, on that dreadful day. My old grand-mother was worried that my father, her only son, had not returned ever since he left the house in the morning, and watched helplessly, as her Bahu (daughter-in-law) was restless and groaning with labour pains.

As my grand-mother tried to pour more oil into the tiny earthen lamp, placed on the window sill, a strong gust of wind threw the small window open and blew out the small earthen lamp frightening everybody in the room. My grandmother somehow closed the window again, and tied it in place, with a handy piece of string. It was now pitch dark in the room; the groping women attending the delivery somehow guessed my arrival, as they were vigilant and experienced. Yes, I had quietly arrived in the midst of all this sound and fury.

All babies, when they are born, cry loudest to herald their arrival. In my case I was modest and unassuming. So, while my grandmother was trying to hunt for a matchbox to relight the lamp, one an elderly and experienced lady, held me safely with her left hand and groped in the dark with her right hand to detect if I was a boy or a girl. Her fingers, it seemed, had some knowledge of Braille, as she announced that a boy was born. But though she shouted *Bhadhaye ho* (congratulations), she was anxious as the newborn produced no sound at all.

The lamp was relit and they noticed the movement of my legs and arms, and were glad to find that I was not a stillborn baby. Yet all the women including my mother and my grandmother showed concern about my silence, and decided to make me cry at any cost, for my own good. So each in her own way, spanked me, slapped my bottom, but being born stubborn, I tolerated the in human reception and uttered no protesting yell, till the pain became intolerable and I groaned a bit audibly – to their satisfaction and to my relief. They were well satisfied.

Surprisingly, being spanked and slapped by my well-wishers has continued all through my life. They have insisted that I should cry for my own good but I have seldom obliged them with such satisfaction. I seemed to have learned to silently lick my own wounds, sitting alone in some remote corner from a dog.

Now, I do not know why, but my mother asked one of the women present "You are sure that my child is a boy? I am asking you Chachi (aunt)." Hearing this, all the women became even more enthusiastic to double check my gender. This was a clear case of "manhandling" by these naughty elderly females, when an innocent infant was caught with his pants down. Now I yelled loudest and they got the hint.

The birth of a male child brought joy to the family. My mother was happy, and my grandmother elated, and the naughty, good natured neighbours were also quite pleased with themselves.

Suddenly the storm subsided, and a loud knock on the door indicated that my father had at last arrived with the village Dayee, Nasiban, who was hurriedly pushed into the room. My father was told to wait outside.

Nasiban, being an experienced Dayee took full control of the situation, and the helpful ladies only had to obey Nasiban's commands. My grandmother, guessing that my father was impatient to know, quickly went out, and without a word clung to him like a little girl checking her sobs. My father, partly frightened, partly anxious, exclaimed "Oh mother say something". My grandmother smiled with tearful eyes and said, "No cause for worry, my dear boy. Listen (making a V for victory sign). Now I have two sons – you and the little brat. Yes Rallia (my father's nickname) You are not alone now, you have a little boy to stand by you... a son to keep you company, when you fight your battles for your rights."

My father said after a little silence. "Thank God, can I see him?" and my grandmother replied, "Not yet... not yet" and she rushed in, closing the door behind.

My father was a handsome young man, educated, but unemployed, and was passing through bad times. About ten months ago he had lost his father, who was quite a personality, a *Raiyees* in his own right. They say my grandfather, Pundit Deen Dayal, was a great horseman who dressed like a Nawab. He rode his white stallion, and enjoyed the best wine. He was tall and much better looking than my Dad. He was respected by the village folk. His sudden death had brought a lot of misery to my friendless, hapless, jobless and penniless father. His own Uncle, a blood relation on my father's side, had thrown him out of the ancestral *Pucca Haveli* (mansion) by procuring some forged documents. This is how my father, by nature meek and gentle, had been tricked, and sent away to pass his days, along with his widowed mother, and an expectant wife, my mother Dhandevi to live in the adjoining mud house.

This wicked Uncle had built a new spacious extension in the compound of the *Haveli*. Daily at dawn he used to sit there with his family members sipping hot tea. This morning, the news of having a 'son' thrilled my father. To express his pride and to demonstrate his vengeance and courage, he walked straight out in the rain, all alone to the courtyard of the 'wicked Uncle', who as usual was sipping hot tea and making fun of my father, who he thought was still chasing the village dayee.

It was still drizzling, though the clouds had allowed a ray of light to penetrate and herald the dawn of a new day. There was a wooden beam, protruding from the wall of this villain's new extension. My father put his shoulder to the beam and pushed it with all his might, and eventually brought down the roof of the extension with a crash. The frightened occupants ran helter-skelter to save their lives. At first they thought it was due to the raging night storm that the roof had given way, but soon they found out that it was actually the doing of a man. The man they had wronged. My triumphant father was shouting at the top of his voice "I am not alone any more, now I have a son. God has sent me two tiny arms as my help – I want justice – I want my share of the ancestral property. Let the world see those forged documents and let the culprit face the law."

And soon a big crowd from the neighbouring houses collected and clapped, they too like the 'Hero' shouted, "Justice has to be done. Our patience too has a limit. This young man has been victimized and denied his share of the property after his father's death".

My grandmother sang her favourite Bhajan (*Nath tunay ghhay kay band chhoraye*). My mother, a good folk singer, sang (*Baraan bindriyan rubba dadhya*). My father attempted to play and sing a 'Ghazal' and I just tried to produce some peculiar sound, "*Bubal, Bubal, Bubal*" and happiness was all pervading.

The bad phase for the Sharma family was over. My father got a job in Amritsar. We rented an apartment with a big room, with a pantry on one side and a kitchen on the other. This was on the third floor of a tall building. There was no house with more than two floors in the area, so ours looked awe-inspiring. Our room had a large window that opened out to the bazaar. I was a toddler now, who wore a long plait of hair like a girl. It was common practice for the Hindu boys in Punjab, to let their hair grow till their *Mundan* Ceremony. I was a fair complexioned chubby child, who hated wearing any clothes but was forced to obey the social norms. I chirped continuously like a bird. My words (rather sounds) never made any sense, but my grandmother always deciphered my warble and often asked me, "Did you mean — Hungry?" I nodded and smiled. Thank God, I was understood by someone.

Hawkers, that yelled in the bazaar to sell their wares, attracted me the most. I noticed that my mother would go to the big window, and waving her hand would beckon the hawkers saying "*Hay bhai they ja*", and I would also join her by shouting, "*Baee de aa...Baee de aa...Baee de aa*", making my yell loud, louder and loudest to show my importance and impatience.

One day my grandmother was in the kitchen and my mother was cleaning the rice, devoting her full attention to her job, when I noticed a hawker in the street selling grapes, which I knew my mother liked to buy everyday. In order to prove helpful, I ran to the big window and then climbed the railing and yelled, "*Baee de aa.*" The hawker ignored my childish yell. So I climbed a little higher, and in my enthusiasm to call the hawker, I lost my balance and toppled over the railing. I would have fallen down like a dead duck on the pavement below, but it was providence that I found I was hanging in mid-air and in a split second might fall down from the third floor window. The fear of death dazed me. I was speechless. I was helpless. My thick plait by chance had got entangled in a long rusty nail that had been fixed by the previous tenant, and which my father had tried many a time to pull out. It had been bent like a hook by the hammering it got from my father.

So hanging precariously, unnoticed and helpless, I seem to have experienced the full impact of imminent death. The human instinct is to stay alive under all circumstances. I did not make any effort to free myself, or cry aloud for help — dazed, I waited for the inevitable to happen at any moment. My chatter having stopped suddenly, and there being complete silence in the room, aroused my grandmother from the kitchen to come to the room. When she noticed the plight of her helpless grandson hanging in the air, as his plait of hair had got entangled in the rusty nail, an intense panic gripped her. But the shocked old lady somehow bent over the railing, and with trembling hands and all her strength tried to pull me up, but failed. Then she shrieked for help and my mother too rushed to the scene. What my mother saw was too shocking for her. She fainted with fright and lay senseless on the floor.

But my grandmother continued her efforts and tugged and toiled and somehow, at last, pulled me into the room, freeing my plait of hair from the rusty nail. Then she placed me on the floor, where my mother lay senseless. Luckily I did not know what fainting was, for me my mother had gone to sleep. I was quite aware of the dramatic happenings and now my concern was the deadly dazed look on my grandmother's frozen face. I somehow felt that I was a culprit and should be properly punished by my elders for my silly act.

To defend myself I managed a pout, but her stare was so frightening that no attempt on my part to move my lips worked. Though I tried to convey: for some kind of a sound — "I am so sorry... I am so silly... I am so stupid". I could not utter any with all my efforts. As the dazed look of my grandmother did not change, I tried a new trick I squeezed my eyes to look more mischievous, but even that had no effect on the stony look of the old lady who sat motionless and frozen. Now my last move was to rush and cling to her neck and sob softly. Soon she too started sobbing; her sobbing appeared more painful, while mine was a bit dramatized. While my mother lay motionless on the floor, we two were sobbing in chorus. Tears flowed from my grandmothers eyes and tears oozed out of mine too. Funny, we human beings express acute pain as well as our overwhelming joy in the same way. Tears tell more than the tongue.

Then my grandmother murmured, "Oh! God you are so merciful, so kind, and you perform miracles that we cannot explain. It was your hand that held Kidar and saved him from a horrible death..." Then she kissed me all over. Both of us had forgotten the third character, my mother, who was lying senseless on the floor in this dramatic situation. All of a sudden my mother regained her consciousness, sat up and looked around and shouted, "Where is my *Kaka* (my boy)?" My grandmother said with wet eyes and a toothless smile, "God has been merciful... he is here without a scratch, saved from the jaws of death." I thought, now my mother would also caress me, but no, she flared up and holding my wrist tightly shouted, "Who told you to go to the window? Next time you go near the railing alone, I shall break all your bones with my own hand." And as if this was not enough, she slapped me, and then hit the wall near her with all her force and then started crying hysterically. My grandmother held her in her embrace and said, "Do not get hysterical, the crisis is over, you are lucky Dhano, very lucky. Kidar is safe and sound... rejoice, our Kidar is reborn today – Dhano – your son is reborn (Dhano was my mother's pet name). You are lucky. Very lucky." Seeing my poor mother crying like a little girl, I approached her and tried to wipe her tears with the sleeve of my shirt. This moved her and howling aloud, "Oh! Kaka" she pulled me closer and embraced me tight and kissed me. I could feel the beating of her heart. God's most wonderful gift to a child is a mother — the greatest gift of God (and poor God never had a mother to embrace).

Prosperity tempted my parents to pamper their chubby child with toys, sweets and goodies of all kind. I was a spoilt brat and my favourite sport was to pick up cups, glasses, spoons and toys that did not interest me and fling them out of the big window from the third floor, and clap with joy on hearing the crashing sounds, while my granny repeated; "That is not good!" My mother would pull my ears and slap me, and that gave me an excuse to run to my father and bury my head in his coat, so that he may pat me and caress me with warmth and understanding. He would often whisper "Women never understand men..." Then wink and I would wink back.

My father's earnings had allowed him to save a substantial amount. My mother advised him to rebuild the old, and decaying mud built portion of the old *Haveli*, that was still our's at Narowal. My grandmother also approved of the idea, and as soon as a thousand was added to his savings of five thousand rupees, the family decided to go back to the village and start the reconstruction work.

Surprisingly, rupees six thousand in 1912 was a large amount of money. My father took leave for a month and he brought us back to Narowal and started the rebuilding work of the part of the ancestral Haveli in our possession, in right earnest.

My grandmother often hugged me and hinted that God was soon going to send a small playmate for me to play with. I could not understand her. "How?" I asked, and her reply was "Just wait." She knew that my mother was expecting another baby. I was now quite a big boy, about 4 years old, but still I was made to wear a bottomless *pajama* (pyjama), as was the custom in those days among the village folk. Of course, my long shirt hid my nudity and I willingly obeyed my elders. Being a healthy, handsome and bright child, I was loved by one and all. They say I was fairer than my father. To me this is now a myth.

One day during a festival, my father took me to the Devi Dwara, Narowal's famous temple, and the priests of the Goddess Durga were thrilled to see me. They were preparing for a *Jhaunki* (tableau) and they needed a small child to enact the role of the naughty Nand Kishore, Lord Krishna as a child. My father readily agreed. I was shown immense love and affection and, thus, did not mind when the old director stripped me and smeared me with blue colour, decorated my forehead with a nice *Tilak*, put a dazzling *mukut* (crown), with peacock feathers, on my head. They surmised that with my long flowing tresses, healthy limbs and charming features, I looked just like Nand Kishore. They had no *pitamber* for me to wear, so my bottomless pajama was dyed yellow and I was made to wear it. I was given a small flute too. They put a big garland of flowers around my neck which covered the front portion of my anatomy, but the cool breeze reminded me of my bare bottom. I, who hated clothes, suddenly felt that clothes and houses were very essential for us human beings, for protection and for privacy.

The *Jhaunki* (Tableau, on the bullock cart) moved with trumpets and bands playing *bhajans* through the streets of Narowal. The crowds approached me with offerings, touched my feet and lowered their heads requesting me for blessings, but I was ill at ease due to my bare bottom.

No sooner had the procession reached our area, I saw my mother and my grandmother looking at me with folded hands and with tears of joy in their eyes. I beckoned to my grandmother, who obliged me by forcing her way through the crowd. As soon as she was near me I jumped from the bullock cart, threw away the flute and mukut in anger and clung to my grandmother. She understood me, and caressing me with her *Dupatta* (veil) scolded my father for offering his son's services as an 'actor'. The management had to select another child to play the part of Nand Kishore and carry on with the procession.

That was the day I told them, that henceforth I would never, ever wear a bottomless pajama. I found to my dismay, that instead of understanding the need of a growing boy and sympathizing with him, they were just amused and kept smiling and nodding silently. Maybe I was too tired or it was time for me to sleep, I just do not remember when I fell asleep in the lap of my grandmother.

Granny and I were the two early birds, while my father and mother slept on till 7:30 or 8:00 am. When I woke up I remembered last night's quarrel and my demand for a proper pajama which all men wear, and the slyness with which my father tried not to comply with my genuine demand. He was more amused than serious about my problem. So when granny was busy in the kitchen that morning, I did a good job with a pair of scissors. That stunned my father since actions speak louder than words. As soon as my father woke up, tried to dress in order to go out he was shocked to find his own pajama with a large hole at the seat. Instead of blowing his top, he picked me up in his arms and said, "You did it?" I nodded, "Yes I did it!" "But, look son." He tried to explain, "I can't go out with a bottomless pajama — I am a man". I whispered, "And so am I". He just stared, and embraced me. And from that day I got proper *pajamas* to wear. Dad was a great friend, a very understanding and loving person.

Time flies fast — my father's leave was almost over, but the construction work still remained incomplete. He had to go back to Amritsar to resume his duties, and my mother badly needed more money. Two days before his departure he took a loan of Rs. 1,500 from a friend, a *Zargar* (ornament maker), to somehow finish the construction work, and mortgaged our part of the haveli for this amount. This Rs. 1,500 brought a lot of trouble and hardship to the family as the interest for the loan went on adding. My father resigned his job as a postman and searched for a new clerical job. He did his best to pay off the loan; he but could not. Destiny's smile had changed into a fearsome frown.

Soon my little sister Guro was born. While my father slogged in Amritsar to support the family and pay the monthly interest, my mother and grandmother somehow managed to survive. I fell sick, very very sick and the chubby child was soon a bundle of bones. The fair skin was tarnished and looked quite dusky. The handsome Kidar Nath became an ugly urchin. Lack of nourishment also made me a dull boy. The only thought that kept me alive was that my father was my best friend, and that I must stand by my best friend and help him to surmount his difficulties. Having found a tenant for the rebuilt *Haveli*, we all moved to Amritsar.

Across our house lived a shop-keeper known for being a miser. He called a carpenter to fix the main door to his dwelling, because the top of the frame had cracked.

A robust argument ensued because the shop-keeper would pay only half a rupee, while the carpenter wanted one. His reason being that an appropriate piece of wood had to be cut to match the area being repaired and then he would have to level the surfaces at a very awkward angle. But the owner was adamant and said, "Just nail the piece of wood, do not level it or do any fancy work, because I shall pay you only half a rupee", as he walked away in a huff. The carpenter started his work. When the shop-keeper was ready to leave for his shop and saw the carpenter levelling the repaired arch, he flew into a rage, "Who the hell told you to do all this. I'll pay no more than half a rupee." The carpenter calmly responded. "You may pay me what you please, but I do not want any one to remark – which idiot did this hack job?"

Troubles never come alone. The firm in which my father was working at that time, M/s Tormal Uttam Chand, suffered heavy losses and the result was total retrenchment. The boss, whom my father served, was helpless; all fifty employees were sacked. When the boss bid my father goodbye, my father said calmly, "No, sir, I shall not quit – you may pay me whatever is convenient and whenever it is convenient. I just cannot serve another boss, or leave my old master alone, when he needs the company of a faithful employee." When my father came home, sad and solemn, and told us about his decision, my mother criticized him cruelly for his folly. She said, "With the family growing, problems, expenses and responsibilities are also multiplying. How are we going to survive?" Surprisingly, my grandmother, who had overheard the argument of the couple, took me aside and confided, "All my life I thought I was useless, ugly, an uneducated village woman with no merit at all. But today, I feel so proud for having brought up your father in this world of selfish people — how many women can have such noble sons? Your father, my son, is a gem of a man. He is so loyal and faithful — promise me you will also be like him — good hearted, truthful and faithful." And she hugged me. I said to her, "Grandma, I wish I could grow up faster and stand by my father." She kissed my forehead and said; "Kidar, I see in you a wonderful man — yes, time will prove it." I told her, "No, no I am not wonderful, I am ugly, thin, poor, timid, and very helpless, but I love my father and my two sisters. To be honest I love Taro more, because she is so nice and good looking and smiles all the time and does not cry like other babies."

Destiny, like a playful prostitute, likes flirting with the life of human beings. She is seldom steadfast. And when she makes prosperity leave by one door, she pushes her uglier stepsister—poverty through the other. And poverty being a sadist and pervert, tramples on the character of her victims. Some become animals and some insane and some drown their sorrow in the bottle. My father in the days, he resigned his job, drank *Tharra* (cheap country liquor) every evening, and returned home quite drunk. This made my mother furious and my grandmother very sad. It puzzled me as I loved my dad as the best friend in the world.

One evening when my father came home, drunk as usual, he was in a very black mood. That day I had a gripping pain in my stomach. I was crying while my mother was rubbing my stomach with hot mustard oil. My father shouted loudest that day. "*Yeh haraamzada kyun row raha hai*?" (Why is this bastard crying?). My grandmother said, "He is not well!" My father retorted, "I shall make him all right." He picked me up and went to the window to open it and throw me out.

The two helpless women rushed forward and pushed him on the bed. They took me away to the kitchen and closed the door, so that my friend could not do the ugly act in his state of drunkenness. Soon my father was fast asleep and the three of us were crying in the kitchen. My father was very sad and ashamed the next morning when he learnt about his devilish acts of the evening before he was very sad and felt ashamed and sorry. He pledged to me "I shall never touch liquor again, never, never", and he never touched the intoxicant for the rest of his life. He kept his word.

CHAPTER 2

"Cheer up – the worse is yet to come." – Philander Johnson

Being a very strong willed child, I reshaped my own destiny, and a great transformation took place. During my school days, when I was eager to study and get an education, my mother one day told me reluctantly, that if I needed further schooling, I would have to earn it myself. She said "With your father's earnings, we can hardly make ends meet." For a boy of seven or eight, it was not easy to earn and learn, but where there is a will there is always a way.

The Pundit Baij Nath High School in Amritsar, where I studied, had started a book binding unit under the guidance of a skilled book binder to help poor students. Volunteering students had to work as book binders for the school library and thus they could earn four *annas* (25 paisas) every day by working for 2 hours daily after school (i.e. from 4 pm. to 6 pm. on weekdays and from 1 pm. to 3 pm. on Saturdays). This helped the poor students financially, but it punished them emotionally.

All boys rich or poor love sports at that age, and like to indulge in their own favourite games in the school play ground. While the sons of the rich enjoyed this luxury, we the children of the poor, slogged in the bookbinding workshop. I was frustrated because I was denied my legitimate right to play games, and instead had to earn a quarter rupee every day. This multiplied by a general sense of deprivation, triggered in me a kind of suppressed anger against the world, which lingers to this day. So if I am told that I am arrogant and assertive, I confess I am — because the seeds were sown when I was a schoolboy. However adversity did me a favour too. It made a man out of a sickly lad. Soon I learnt that clowning was a good remedy for heartaches, backaches and headaches. I developed, like my father, a great sense of humour which has proved very useful.

My loneliness taught me philosophy and my creative urge awakened the poet in me. My father's passion for music, was inherited by me and that helped to make life worth living under all conditions. I consoled myself with the thought, that, maybe God had knowingly made me ugly and funny, to amuse his favourite children – children born to rich families. So I compromised with my destiny.

Now, in our bookbinding unit, we had a small boy called Yousaf, who was perhaps the poorest of us all, but who was always smiling and whistling. *The happiest people seem to be those who have no particular reason for being happy, except that they are so. – William R. Inge*

He was younger to me, and we became good friends.

He told me one day that he was an orphan and that his parents had died when he was barely four years old. He lived now with his sick and aged grandmother, and that he had to go home after his bookbinding work and cook the evening meals for both of them.

One day he made me cry by showing me his greatest treasure, which he always carried with him, in a small old worn out purse. He opened the purse, when we were alone in the room. "Look", he said with deep pride, "this button is from the *sherwani* (long coat) of my father, and this broken piece of glass bangle belonged to my mother – with these belongings in my pocket, I carry my parents with me wherever I go. I don't show these articles to anyone, not even to my granny, because then she weeps and weeps. I have learned to stop weeping for the last one year, my stock of tears is exhausted. I hope God knows about it — or maybe he does not — who cares? He must be a friend of the rich, so unlike you and me, he does not have to do bookbinding." Yousaf laughed.

I decided to be more helpful to my young friend Yousaf and told him that he could work for just one hour only and could leave his unfinished jobs to me to complete. Being far more skilled as a bookbinder than any other boy in the unit, I could complete more books in half the time. I saved a full hour for Yousaf so that he could go home and cook for his grandmother and himself. I thought if I did a good turn to a fellow student each day, then maybe my ugliness would change to charm. I longed to be handsome like my dad, but I was dark and ugly.

Winters in Punjab are very severe. The temperature during winter touches sub-zero. During December and January, while working late in the bookbinding workshop, my fingers would get frozen when I dipped them into the ice-cold paste. When the winter rains started, the punishment for the poor intensified. Neither Yousaf nor I had an umbrella, and one day Yousaf did not dare go out in the rain in his torn old garments. So as soon as the rain abated a little, we both left the workshop, promising the Instructor we would complete our job the next day, which being a Saturday would give us more hours to work.

That was the last time I saw my buddy, the cheerful whistling Yousaf, because that night, due to the heavy rains, their old house collapsed, killing my young friend and his grandmother. God writes such cruel short stories, I thought. This news reached us on Monday and made me disconsolate. I had to struggle very hard to hold back the gushing tears. Silently, I slipped away to the school washroom, closed the door and cried and cried till my eyes began to hurt.

I could no longer attend the bookbinding workshop because Yousaf's memory haunted me. His innocent, smiling face and his funny pout, while whistling a tune, lingered in my memory. I told my grandmother the entire sad story of Yousaf and confessed that henceforth I would no longer be able to attend the bookbinding workshop and earn the daily wage of four annas. She said, "Do not worry son, when one door is closed, God opens the other door — you will see, some miracle will happen soon".

And it did happen. My father's rich uncle Pundit Kirpa Ram, the elder brother of the wicked uncle Gukal Das of Narowal, all of a sudden arrived from Multan and decided to live permanently in Amritsar . He was once in the Army, and after retirement practised medicine (Unani) and was a very capable *Hakeem*. He was quite rich and his practice earned him about six to seven hundred rupees a month.

He took a three — room flat, of his own choice, with the help of an old friend, who was a resident of Amritsar. Pundit Kirpa Ram was a bachelor, and a very kind hearted. When he saw me he liked me very much. He had an old servant who looked after him and cooked his meals. My father insisted that henceforth, since he took only one evening meal a day, he (my father) would see that his children, Kidar Nath or Guro or Taro would bring him a hot meal in a tiffin carrier every evening. Pundit Kirparam our *Dadajee* (grandfather) agreed. So daily, Taro, who was too young to carry any load, walked with me to his flat and delivered his hot meals. He was so pleased with us that he gave us lots of fruits and sweets and immense love. As granny had predicted, when the earnings from the bookbinding unit stopped, Dadajee – the old angel – gave me the cash so I could continue my studies comfortably. He even prompted me to develop some hobby — such as writing, painting or even photography. I was excited most by the third option, photography, so when I told him that a Brownie box camera would cost Rs. 15 he readily gave me Rs. 40 to buy a superior camera. I was very thrilled and the whole family was grateful to the gracious old gentleman, who helped everyone in the Sharma family.

Three years passed like three weeks. But one evening when Taro and I reached his house with the evening meals the servant told us that his old master had died, and that I should run back immediately and inform my parents about the tragedy. So, Taro and I, ran home sobbing. My father, my mother and my grandmother were all overwhelmed by his death, and his last rites were performed as if my Dad had lost his own father once again. With the death of Dadajee, adversity once again took charge of our life with added vengeance.

The hardships grew, and so did the family. Ragunath was born, a charming little chap who was very, very handsome and gentle. Whether he was awake or asleep, there was always a sunny smile on his rosy lips. He was hardly two years old when he had fever one evening, and by the next dawn Ragunath was dead. The whole family could not bear the shock. Everyone wept and nobody could touch a morsel that fateful day. Every one tried to guess, what had happened to the child but no one could find the real reason.

Next year God sent Vishwa a duplicate of Ragunath, but like his elder brother, he too died in identical circumstances. I think the two shrewd fellows had guessed correctly that the family was going through very hard times, and instead of being a burden, it was wiser to return hastily 'thither, whence they had come'.

After their deaths another tragedy awaited us. Taro my younger sister fell sick. It was just a bad cold and the usual temperature accompanied it. The doctor pronounced it as a mild case of flu. But destiny had other plans and the fever though not very high, persisted. Taro was bedridden for more than two months. Again it was because of poverty, lack of proper nourishment and inadequate medical help that she developed tuberculosis. In those days TB, plague and small pox, had no known cure.

The eyes of a TB patient become large as the face gets sunken. When I asked Taro why her lotus eyes were getting bigger and bigger she said: "My eyes are hungry and want to devour as much as possible in a short time." Taro tried to the last moment not to be a problem for the family. She would tell granny with a smile that as soon as spring came, she would be on her feet again. '*Bus koil ko boolne doe us paad pur*' (Let the cuckoo sing once again on yonder tree). Spring was just a few weeks away, when one wintry night, just before dawn, when everyone was fast asleep, I heard Taro calling for my mother and before I could get up to wake her, my mother had already rushed to Taro's bed. She said in a soft voice "Yes dear, do you need anything?" Taro with her usual wit replied "Only one thing — you mama — the most precious thing on earth — you." My mother holding her warm hand said: "Yes, I am at your service my pet! Tell me what should I do for you?"

Taro after a short silence, tried to smile painfully and said in a faint voice, which I was very attentive to hear. She said "Mama, time has come for me to take leave of you and my last wish is that some lines from the Gita be recited, as a ritual for the departing soul. But mama I know you never went to school and granny too is illiterate, but can one of your dear friends, your favourite *sahelies* (friends) Jumuna and Paro Aunty, who are both so religious and pious, can they come to your dying daughter's help. So, please just see that one of these two *bhagtanees* (devout people) come to my help and just read a few lines of the sacred scripture near my bed – could you please see if that is possible?"

So my mother with a lump in her throat, wiping her eyes left on tip toe to bring one of the two *sahelies* to fulfil her daughter's dying wish. But she was mistaken. People do not help us when we need help badly, they do when it suits them. Both these ultra religious and pious ladies refused to come, declaring that it was most unsafe to go near a person dying of tuberculosis. My simple illiterate mother shocked, heartbroken and defeated in her mission returned home to Taro, and in a tearful voice told her daughter what the pious ladies had said. Then my mother suggested that maybe my father could do something. But Taro said, "Please do not wake up father, he worked very hard last night and slept very late and besides he too knows only Urdu and English and not Sanskrit."

Before my poor sister could speak another word, I jumped to my feet and approaching her said "Taro, look. I can read the Gita, my teacher taught me in school — but my problem is that I cannot read it aloud.' "That does not matter", said Taro. "Gita recited is Gita recitation, and it makes me proud that my own dear brother is fulfilling my last wish." Actually I was telling a white lie. God above knows, I had never read a line of the Gita nor ever really heard any one reading it to me. I only wanted my sister to have some peace of mind and the satisfaction that the Scripture were read near her bed when she left this cruel world. So with a heavy heart I took a book of Algebra in my hand, I pretended to read the sacred lines from the Gita. This not only made my sister happy, but it impressed my simple mother too who looked at her Kidar Nath with renewed pride. I acted, trying to sway, making gestures with my hands, like Sanskrit scholars do, while performing holy *Yagnas*.

Actually I was cheating my mother and her dying daughter, my own dear sister who trusted me so much. I was cheating God Almighty too. I was a liar, a cheat a fraud. Soon, giving me a last look of thankfulness, my sister, the young lady with the lotus eyes closed her lids, never to open them again. She died peacefully with a smile on her face. My mother bent over Taro's dead body and kissed her, again and again, and at last she shrieked aloud with agony and every one knew that the inevitable had happened. That Taro had at last left on her long journey. My father said crying "Taro, I have been denied decorating your *Doli* (bridal vehicle) but I will decorate your *Arrthi* (funeral vehicle)... my pet child."

I do not know if God ever pardoned me for my blatant lie that night, but I do know that I and the Almighty are not on speaking terms. And I do not know who is feeling more guilty, I or the Creator of this awful world. Any way that was my first major lie, and many more have followed later in life. Lies, lies and more lies. Death alone is the real truth. Death is the soothing silent mother. Her child may be a sinner or a saint but once he sleeps in her lap, she accepts and adores her child.

Chapter 3

"It is better to wear out, than to rust out."

Richard Cumberland

Time marched on. The year was 1925, and I was preparing for my eighth standard university exam. It was called middle-class and it was not a school exam, but a university examination. Any student who stood first in the district was awarded a scholarship of Rs. 50 per month for two years. I had no hope of ever winning a scholarship because my prescribed books were second hand, which I had bought with great difficulty, and they had a chapter or two missing in the beginning, and some pages missing at the end . Also I did not have time to study since I had to pay for my tuition by painting signboards and making kites.

Another change that I was going through was the change from a lad to a man — puberty. Nature with her five year plan had already started the transformation. Signs of adolescence started showing all over my body. This created some new ticklish problems for the meek and shy Brahmin boy. Whiskers were visible on my upper lip and somehow the feminine form started appearing very attractive to me. A young girl's smile was unbearably alluring, invisible magnetism pulled me to each and every young girl that I met on the street. But being a timid young man, it was I who blushed, instead of the girls passing me by, and if a group of girls read my thoughts they were eloquent, in passing very appropriate remarks, and that made me hide my face in shame. I was now lost mostly in amorous day dreams from morning to night. I wanted to hold the pretty hands of some neighbouring beauties, but lacked the courage to even address them and say hello. It is the age when your hormones are doing the thinking, not your brain.

My father who could not earn enough, started borrowing. Practice makes a man perfect and my father had acquired great skill in the art of borrowing money and writing any kind of promissory note desired by the money lenders. There was hardly enough food for the family and the addition of a baby boy, my younger brother Himmat Rai, did not help matters, and he had to go without milk many a time.

One day my father borrowed Rs. 100 and bought an excellent harmonium for his dear son Kidar Nath to learn to play. This would satisfy my father's love of music. I also loved music and became an expert harmonium player. I played, not only to please my music loving father, but, I also started giving tuitions to boys and girls of well-to-do families in the art of playing the harmonium — that wonderful musical instrument of those days. Not only was I a good harmonium player, I was also an amateur photographer. I was a Jack-of-all-trades but a master-of-none. While my father tried hard to support the family, it was left to me to earn the necessary money for continuing my studies. So I did many part time jobs, I was a harmonium teacher, a sign painter, a book binder, a drawing instructor, and so was fully occupied from early in the morning to late at night.

I vividly remember to this day, how once on Dewali day when I returned home from my tuition, I found to my surprise that ours was the only house in the neighbourhood which was plunged in total darkness. The whole city, each and every corner of the town was bright with lamps, candles and decorative bulbs. Years later I was able to express my experience when I wrote "*Row di shamma fasurda, tootay falak say taaray, dhhoraiya ja raha hai shayad mera afsaana*" (The sad flame started a-weeping, and stars fell from the skies perhaps my tale was being retold). I was puzzled and asked my mother why she was not celebrating Dewali, the annual festival of lights. My mother, in a very sad tone, said "There is no money in the house and your father went out to borrow some cash from some of his good old friends. I think he is still chasing his good friends for a loan, or may be the good old friends are searching for extra money to help your father on Dewali day".

I understood her and in the darkness I read the faces of my sister Guro, who was quite grown up now and my younger brother Himmat, who whenever he needed anything badly, would cling to my legs. He clung to my legs and said, "I want fire crackers" in his lispy voice. I was woefully sad and pondered for a while, what to do to bring some light into this house. I had started painting a portrait of Lord Ram, a few days ago. I took it down to look at it under the lamp post and hurriedly put some finishing touches to it, on the footpath. Then I took it to my friend Fazlu the frame maker. I got it framed on credit and soon the 'master piece' was ready for sale.

I had to sell it, and sell it soon, but I did not know how to do so. In the area near my house and P.N.B. school, people knew me, so I decided to go to *Namuk Manndi* (salt market) to sell my painting of Lord Rama on Dewali day. Now I did not know how to hawk my painting. I just held it, exhibiting it to the passers by and walked up and down the street. In this crowded street, people stopped, looked at my painting but no one asked whether it was for sale. I whispered to the smiling picture of the Lord "God you are for sale tonight, I wonder if you will get a customer?"

At last I shifted from this area to another bazaar, but no luck. I was tired and hungry and heartbroken, worried how I would pay Fazlu the frame maker who had helped me with a frame of my choice, on credit. Suddenly an elderly gentleman came and stopped me. He looked at my painting with keen interest for a long time, then asked, "For how much did you buy this beautiful picture?" I replied, "I am selling this beautiful picture and that too for a song!" He asked me, "how much?" I replied, " Not less than ten rupees". He said, "Ten — no...no, I shall pay you fifteen rupees and gladly too." He paid cash, and carrying the frame with great reverence, walked away with the portrait of the smiling Rama giving me a last look. I sat in a lonely corner, looked at the money and cried with joy. This was the poor painter's first victory. With fifteen rupees in those days you could buy anything! I paid four rupees for the frame to Fazlu and for six rupees, I bought two kilos of sweets of excellent quality and spent two on candles and one on fire crackers for Himmat. And with two rupees still in my pocket, hard cash, I ran home as quickly as possible.

That was the happiest Dewali we celebrated. Little Himmat danced and Guro sang and my mother smiled and my grandmother cried with joy. There was however one person in this family who remained mum and continued puffing away at his *Hukka* (hubble- bubble). That was my dear father. He was pensive, he was morose, and he felt defeated, because what he had failed to do, his son Kidar had done. I noticed my father's reaction and when nobody was around. I asked, "Have I done anything wrong?" His reply was, "No, no, you have been wonderful and I am proud of you. I am heartbroken because all my friends let me down tonight." I said with a smile, "Not all Dad", and he got the hint and embraced me and said, "Now let us hear you play on the harmonium my favourite song *Ajab hairaan hun Bhagwan* and let Guro sing it aloud." And my mother said, "and I shall play the *Dholak* (drums)." She was a great *dholak* player and had a very good sense of rhythm. Fortunately for me, as the saying goes, "Like mother like son." And every body was overjoyed that Dewali night. I had bought ecstasy for all the family with just thirteen rupees. "The art of life is to know how to enjoy a little and to endure much" — William Hazlitt.

Going back a bit to my father's favourite song, I wish to reproduce a part of Pandit Betaab's writing, *"Ajab hairaan hun bhagwan, tumhe kiyun kur rijhaoon main, koye vastu nahin aaise jisse seva main laon main— tumhi ho moorti mayn bhi, tumhi vyapak ho phoolon main, bhalla bhagwan ko bhagwan pay kaise chharoon main— tumharee jyoti say rowshan hain, sooraj chaand aur taarey, maha aandher hai tujhko agar deepak dikhaon main"* (God I am bewildered as to how to please or gladden You, There isn't a thing I can put to such use. – You are enshrined in the statue and manifest in the flowers, how can I offer God to God? – Your effulgence illuminates the sun, moon and stars. It is not the darkest gloom to hold a candle up to You!)

My second unexpected victory that year was winning a scholarship. I had stood first. So the first instalment was three crisp new five rupee notes which my headmaster gave me saying, "We are proud of you Kidar". With joy in my heart, a song on my lips and fifteen rupees in my pocket, I reached home and gave my family the good news. My father just touched the money and said "*Yaar tu nay to kamaal kur deeiya*." (My dear friend you have done a wonderful job). He always addressed me as *yaar* whenever he had to express his love. Then he whispered, "Show these crisp notes to my mother first and then your own mother."

So I took the money to my grandmother and told her about my winning a scholarship. Her remark was "I do not understand what a stollertip is just say *Inam* (prize)." And I said, "Yes *Inam*". She held the money in her hand kissed it and said "May God bless you and may you win more Inams!" Then I told her that she was to accept one of the five rupee notes, as a present from her grandson Kidar. With rare pride, which only old people know to express with a smile, liquid eyes and trembling voice, granny said, "Young man, what will an old woman of my age do with this immense fortune? — Five rupees!, no, no son, just give me one silver coin, just give me one rupee, I am old fashioned, I like silver." I replied, "No, you have to accept my humble present, I am giving you one five rupee note and one to my mother and one to my younger sister Guro and younger brother — Himmat." "And what about you?" she inquired. I told her that every month I would be getting three five rupee notes for the next two years. So, she accepted the fiver and touching it to her forehead said, "This is the second time in my life that I am given five rupees as a present. Long ago, a loving male, your grandfather when he brought me home to Narowal as a bride, gave me five rupees. Then he had said 'Bhagan — must dance now,' and I did dance, I was so overwhelmed with joy. I am overwhelmed with joy today too and I will dance for you, I do not know if my worn legs will allow me, but if you wish I will try." I just clung to her and we both cried with happiness. Time seemed to have stopped just for a few moments that day. Then she wiped her eyes and mine and said, "Let me go straight to the temple and tell *Thakurji* (the deity) about your *Inam* and about my pride, my joy and my gratitude"

In those days society was full of simple folk, who kept no secrets from their gods in the temples. They thought, like my grandmother, that these gods and goddesses were the senior members of their own family and nothing should be hidden from them. Today people, young and old are much more sophisticated more advanced and avoid such innocent and honest interactions.

Two years after, this incident my grandmother left for her heavenly abode. Without making any fuss about her departure, she slept one night and never woke up again. After her cremation, my father opened her wooden box and found that five rupee note wrapped carefully in a silken scarf. This conveyed to me my grandmother's idea of love. She used to say, "Love is carefully treasuring the gift given to you by your beloved," thus treasuring my humble gift to her, till her dying day. Granny was an illiterate and a simple soul. She was my 'Guru', my great teacher in many ways. She had taught me a *Bhajan* (hymn) – "*Naath tu nay ghhaj ke bandh chhoray*" (Lord, you protected the helpless elephant caught in the jaws of a wicked crocodile...) She said this *Bhajan* was a prayer, a kind of SOS to God, and whenever it is recited with faith and sincerity, it would always help find a way out. "Prayer does not change God, but it changes him who prays." – Soren Kierkegaard.

The other words of wisdom my grandmother had whispered in my ears were, "A real temple, big or small is a birthday present to the Lord — make your heart a temple and the Lord will always be there." Today I believe that the Almighty Master is only a whisper away. And whenever I have sincerely reached out for help, the response has been amazingly fast. For, has He not protected me from so many dangerous situations?

Chapter 4

"In the firmament He set the stars, and in the mind of man — Will."

The one luxury, which I did not deny myself despite my poverty, was the luxury of kite flying. Maybe this habit of looking up has made me what I am today. I could not afford to buy kites so I made my own. Being a skilled bookbinder, my fingers knew the use of paste, and my skill as a painter made the artist in me create my own designs. I used to buy thin paper sheets of different colours and make two dozen kites of different shapes and designs on Saturday night. Then on Sunday morning, with an army of children as followers and aides, I enjoyed the thrill of kite flying.

My father often joined me and once I made a giant kite which was about ten feet by ten feet. It was made of thick brown wrapping paper. Everybody was of the opinion that this kite was just a show piece and would never fly. But I had worked out all the details. Instead of using the usual string I managed to get a thick strong cord. My father showed more interest than me in this experiment. He even joined me as my assistant the day the kite was ready for its first flight. My playmates also assembled to assist me in my adventure. My great kite responded and it was soon ascending the sky. It was a sight that brought many people to their house tops. Soon the neighbourhood was crowded with an audience to watch my big kite, as it hissed aloud and soared up and up in the sky.

As soon as it was airborne, it showed off its stature with a brisk hissing sound. The wind now caught it and pulled it so hard it became difficult for me to keep my feet on the ground. Yes, it pulled me with such force that my father had to hold on to me firmly to keep me from flying away. But the thrill and fun were short lived, the thick cord that I had used, snapped and my big kite, like a dream drifted away over the distant house tops, never to be seen again. Everyone moved away disappointed, but my father and I stood there for a long time and then my father muttered, "The bigger the dream, the larger the disappointment." I never attempted to fly a kite again, ever.

Lahore was much more important than the humble city of Amritsar. It was the Paris of Punjab. Occasionally as a group, we students would travel to Lahore for stimulus and excitement. On one of these trips, my friend and I entered a hall in Anarkali bazaar, to enjoy a symposium on Punjabi poetry being presided over by the Minister Chowdhury Shabbudin. The winner was to get a gold medal. As was to be expected, most of the audience were Sardarjees, and so were the older and senior competitors. After listening for a while, I sent a note to the president, "*Motian walio zara ik shagird nu wee mouka davo*". Chowdhury Sahib was amused by my message and invited me to recite my writing in Punjabi. I recited what I consider, one of my outstanding works in creating pictorial imagery with words, "*Utter kaanto main chhadan*", which on request I was forced to repeat at many subsequent gatherings.

There was stunned silence in the audience, and shock amongst the competitors as I recited. This was followed by thunderous, prolonged applause, leaving only one winner. When I reached home, I told my father, who reacted with the words, "You are a bluffer, and a storyteller. Who will give you a gold medal?" When I showed and offered it to him, he declined saying that I should keep it as a souvenir of my achievement.

In 1927 my sister Guro was married and she left us to go and live with her in-laws. That same year I passed my matriculation examination. I won a scholarship once again, standing first in the University. My father's ambition was, for me to get a Master of Arts degree and then a Ph. D. so that he could boast that his son Kidar Nath was a M.A. Ph. D. His secret desire was that I should be a professor or a principal in a college. So the day my results were out, he somehow managed to get three hundred rupees and gave me the money saying, "Here, friend, this is for your college fees, admission, and the necessary books. I hope it will be sufficient." It was more than sufficient. He wanted me to shake hands with him. My mother was against any further education and suggested that having matriculated, I should get a job in a bank or in an office like her elder brothers and be helpful to my poor father. But my father winked and whispered, "Don't listen to this woman — go ahead with your studies."

My father had his own ambitions for me, while my mother had her own plans also, but no one knew about my secret desires, – I wanted to join the films and be a "dream merchant". Prose, poetry, painting, music, dance, movement and all the visual arts fused into 'one overwhelming experience'. To me Cinema was a brilliant, multifaceted diamond, which thrilled my whole being.

In those days, Cinema was a poor man's source of entertainment, and it still is today, while theatre was for the elite. Movies had learned to move, but the images on the silver screen were silent. To minimize the monotony, the cinema owners used to engage local musicians, who got close to the screen and played hybrid tunes, to match the projected images on the screen. Sometimes they added gusto to the ordinary scenario, with well-synchronized sound effects.

In Punjab, the musicians always played their own favourite tune '*Hay jammalo*' when the film was nearing the end. This tune was played more vigorously if the film was enjoyable. The audience too, thumped their feet in rhythm to indicate that they had enjoyed the movie, otherwise, as soon as the '*Hay jammalo*' tune started, people got up to leave, not bothering to wait for the last "The end" title. Foreign movies had subtitles in English to tell the audience what the characters were saying, or what the filmmaker intended to convey. Surprisingly even those who could not read English were able to sense correctly what was happening. Tickets cost four annas for the 'popular class', to which students and the general public belonged, because that was what we could afford. No one bothered about the queue system. First come, first served was the motto, and might is right was the practice. To buy a ticket I had to first remove my shirt, to protect it from getting torn in the struggle, and I pushed my fist with the coins in my hand through the box office window while many other hands were attempting the same thing. Being thin but energetic I always managed to buy tickets for my self as well as for some of my friends. Afterwards I tended to my bruises, or occasionally, the oozing blood. I always occupied a front row seat in the cinema hall. There were no printed photographs or film magazines in those days, but the cinema operators sold some celluloid frames, usually close-ups of famous Indian and Hollywood actors like Vithal or Kajan Bai, Eddie Polo and Elmo Lincoln. These mighty stars were the heroes, that all youngsters worshipped. I bought many frames of these stars and showed them to my friends with great pride.

Cinema, the new art form, fascinated me so much that I ran away from home with the money that my father had given me for my college education. Me and my friend, philosopher, and guide Master Gurdit Singh. He was my art & drawing teacher. We bought two third class railway tickets to go to Bombay – the Hollywood of Indian Cinema. I told my drawing teacher to write a note to my father saying, "Please Punditji do not worry. Kidar and I are going to Bombay to try our luck in films. Kidar Nath has dreams of becoming a Dream Merchant, and I am going to help him achieve his goal. I am positive that the young man is sure to surprise everybody some day." My father was furious when he got the note, but since there was no address, he was unable to contact us.

This was my first adventure, as a young lad. I was travelling hundreds of miles away from home and in those days, Bombay was regarded by the simple people of Punjab as *Pardes* (a foreign land).

The train stopped at a remote, desolate station. I saw a little girl of four years carrying a three year old child and inquired, "Is your burden not too heavy?" She innocently replied, " How can brothers ever be a burden."

I had in my black steel trunk, carefully packed, a film story, written by me in English which I knew was going to be my springboard to fame and fortune. I believed like all other story writers that my story was a sure hit. I also carried with me my brownie box camera. A new camera that took beautiful photographs. This camera won me friends quicker than my screen stories. We travelled by third class, and even after crossing Delhi, our compartment was still quite empty. The reason being the sight of my companion a real Sardarji with a beard and turban, and me a skinny Punjabi, unnerved the passengers. At every station, when they peeped into our compartment, and finding us comfortably lying on the berths must have thought to themselves, "Let sleeping Punjabis lie."

Though the journey was long and tiring, I was excited as I watched the changing scenery. When we reached Ratlam, it started raining heavily and suddenly the lights in the compartment become dim. A Gujarati family of four, a meek husband, a huge domineering wife, a delicate and cute looking teenage daughter and a nice looking little boy, hurriedly pushed their luggage into our compartment. We politely welcomed them and helped them with their several suitcases, bedding and baskets. When the train started with a jerk, the delicate husband fell into Master Gurdit Singh's lap and the little boy clung to my legs for support while the two ladies, one big and the other small, held on to each other.

Slowly the two ladies found their seats and when the lights got brighter we could see each other. Gurdit Singh was politely telling the husband, who had fallen into this lap, "*Koye baat nahin, baitho baitho*." (It is all right you may keep sitting). The Gujarati gentleman, discovering that his benefactor was a burly, bearded Punjabi Sikh at once jumped to his feet and begging Sardarji's pardon, moved over to his protective wife. The little boy sat by my side. Soon the sky became brighter, the rain was only a drizzle and the Gujarati girl appeared to me as a 'Princess' in dreamland. Though I wanted to stare at her constantly, I just managed to cast my glances down and looked at her occasionally out of the corner of my eyes.

At the next station, the Gujarati family got down to have their tea, and the gentleman asked us if we would like some too. We both said in a chorus, "No tea — we take milk!" The girl laughed, the mother frowned and the little boy pulled his father away.

When they came back they preferred to sit on the opposite berth and discuss their own problems in Gujarati. To attract the girl's attention I took out my loaded camera and started fiddling with it. Today every Tom, Dick and Harry carries a portable camera, but in those days to own a camera was a privilege and I considered myself one of the chosen few.

The trick worked, the young boy came to me and the girl said in Gujarati, "*Tame maaro ani Parveen no photo paaro*" (Can you take a photograph of me and Parveen?)

I was a little baffled because the word paaro means to tear or rip in Punjabi, but I soon guessed her meaning. I suggested that I would take the boy's picture first and then the whole family. His sister adjusted Parveen's hair with her fingers and made him wear her loose ring but instructed him to be careful. As the film in those days was slow, I asked the boy to stand near the door of the moving train, not realizing that the door of the train opened outwards. As I was focusing the camera, the train jolted and suddenly Parveen disappeared from my ground glass view finder. With the jolt, the door was flung open and Parveen who was holding it, flew out of the compartment in a split second. The mother shrieked and my companion and the boy's father pulled the emergency chain with all their might. The charming young lady started crying, and the dominating woman pointed her finger at me, and accused me of throwing her son out of the moving train.

I was puzzled, and for help looked at the charming young lady. To my consternation, she too nodded and confirmed her mother's accusation. She also shouted "You murderer! why did you do it?" Now I learned that beauty has fangs also. I was frightened and speechless. I did not know how to defend myself. I was fully aware of the punishment for murder, and

I knew how the British Government in those days hanged the guilty. I began to perspire. The train came to a halt with a screech, the father and Gurdit Singh jumped down and ran in the direction where the child had fallen.

I was expecting some Railway Policeman to come and arrest me. Except for me, no one bothered to realize that it was an accident and that I was quite innocent. I felt that I was alone, defenceless, helpless and speechless. Then I waited for the 'fade in' of the next scene in this real life drama. Destiny the master of suspense, had a pleasant surprise for all of us.

The Parsi Guard of the train arrived on the scene, carrying Parveen in one piece in his arms and said, "Here is our little Tarzan, who jumped for fun from the train. Luckily the ground was soft due to the heavy rain and the long green grass saved him". This miracle amazed everybody, the parents were overjoyed and I was relieved.

Parveen's father addressed me and I did not know why he said it to me, "Isn't God great? Not a scratch, my son is safe and sound". I was still carrying a grudge against God ever since my sister Taro's death, but now I regained my faith in the Almighty. I went to the toilet to cry alone. I don't like to be seen with tears in my eyes. I closed my eyes and thanked my Maker for finding some time from his busy schedule to save little Parveen from injury and Kidar Nath from handcuffs.

We reached Bombay at last, I was dazed to see the grandeur of the big city. Master Gurdit Singh on the advice of one of his relatives, who had visited the city several times, engaged a Victoria or horse buggy, and we reached Kalbadevi area where we found a *Dharamshala* (lodging house). We were given two wooden boxes in which to keep our luggage. These we locked up safely. Then after a bath we had a hot meal at a nearby *Dhaba* (street stall). We were in no mood to have a nap; we wanted to explore the enchanting city. We walked aimlessly in the crowded streets and then enjoyed a ride in the tram car. At night we spread our bedding on the floor of the big central hall and had a very sound sleep.

Next day we set out to see more of the city and we visited the Gateway of India. When we reached there, I was overwhelmed to see the tossing waves of the ocean, I had never seen the sea. Years later I wrote, "*Madhukar mahfil sooni thi, taaron nay aa kay bhar dee kiyun, chhand nay saagar kay seenay main dharkan paida kur dee kiyun.*" (Madhukar, why was your desolate assembly peopled by the stars, And why has the moon created a throbbing in the bosom of the ocean).

We even ventured a ride in a steam boat. I looked back to see the Gateway of India from a long distance with the Taj Mahal Hotel in the background. When we returned to the Gateway of India, the area was full of various types of people: Parsis, Muslims, Hindus, Christians and foreigners. The sight that captivated me the most was the *kashta* style sari (nine yards of sari) worn by the Maharastrian women, beautifully draped to reveal their curves.

In Punjab the Muslim women mostly wore a *burkha*, and the rest of them were heavily draped. Being a Punjabi who had never seen the posterior of a woman, I was on cloud nine. Their alluring backs and the variety of shapes and sizes of the women intoxicated us both. Being young and distracted by their curves, in my excitement I got separated from my companion. I walked aimlessly on, behind a fisher-women, whose style of wearing the *kashta* sari made me blush since it exposed the hip line much more clearly. My interest was not in the fish she was selling but in her anatomy, and I changed the path in which I was headed, and followed her as closely as possible. She noticed me and sensing I was stranger to the city, asked me by using gestures if I wanted to buy fish. I blushed, nodded and handed her a Rs.10 note. She sat down, I could now see her stiff form from a top angle. She pulled out her purse from her blouse revealing a rich feminine form and gave me a rupee back, handed me a dead fish, and again using gestures conveyed to me, "Now, get lost".

She was soon lost in the crowd and the Brahmin boy did not know what to do with the dead fish and the awful stink. I walked back to the Gateway of India and threw the fish back in the Arabian sea. To tell you the truth, such idiosyncrasies of youth, make life more interesting than the rewards of wisdom that come with age and experience.

Like all school boys, who have the wrong notion about their ability and talent, I too imagined that I was a brilliant writer, an excellent lyricist, and was born, like the great masters and great artists, to scale great heights in the art of 'Film Making' in my country. All I needed was a start and I was now in Bollywood, the Mecca of Indian movies.

My companion and I visited all the studios and whoever we met on the studio premises – whether a tailor, a make-up man or even the boy who just served tea or coffee. I tried to impress them, with my screenplays which I had laboured so hard to complete. They patiently listened for some time and then making an excuse went their way, never to be seen again. They even lifted their little finger while I was in mid-sentence, which in Bombay indicates the urgent need to go to the toilet.

Disgusted with this thoughtlessness, I often looked heavenwards of course, and uttered a variation of the famous words of the sages: "God, please forgive them for they know not what they are missing". My companion who had all the faith in me, joined in the chorus with, "Pardon these fools" in an even louder voice.

I visited many studios, managed to get a few meetings with the top brass, but none of them could see the flame burning in the heart of the boy from Punjab. All I wanted was one chance to show my worth but there were no willing takers.

I pleaded with them that I had an excellent moral character, that I was a vegetarian and boasted that I was even a virgin, but alas, they either laughed at me politely or showed me the door. I was crestfallen, dejected, disappointed and defeated. I consoled myself, recalling the fate of some of the greatest masters, as recorded by history, who were largely ignored by their own countrymen, until after their death. I was determined to change my destiny from these former greats. I could not wait till after death. Finally, with dwindling cash and no hope to persuade this cruel city, we headed back to Amritsar. When at last the prodigal son returned home, my father was furious and used many kinds of different words in Punjabi, Hindi, Urdu, and even in crude English, all of which conveyed: "Rascal, you are a worthless fellow, you betrayed my trust, wasted my money, and made a fool out of yourself."

When the drama reached a high pitch, my mother interrupted him and intervened. Her sobbing and crying overwhelmed my father. Soon the wolf was a lamb and his last words, as he left the room, were, "Ask him if he is hungry?" I was very hungry and was glad to be given a hot meal.

Next morning, while my father was still in bed I went over and, gently touching his feet implored him — "I want to join college, Dad". He paused for a while and said, "This time I am personally going with you to see that you get admitted in the Hindu Sabha College". I was admitted when the vice-principal moved by my father's affection, not only pardoned me, but once again arranged cash for my higher education. I joined the college and tried to forget about movies and films, and my last trip to Bombay. When my friends and my professors, who liked me for my pen and brush, inquired about my adventure in Bombay, I bragged a bit but said, "It is not a nice profession for people like you and me, people with high moral standards. It is only for the Bhands. " My father's pet phrase for low character entertainers.

Two of my professors in college became close friends. Prof. Vishnudutt, my physics professor, who was extremely intelligent, and soft like silk but hard as steel. He liked me for my wit, my skill in poetry and music. He was very fond of music but could not sing. His wife had an excellent ear for music.

My other teacher was Prof. Mathur, who was also crazy about music. He played the Sarangi, and his wife was accomplished in playing the *Dholak*. I accompanied them playing the harmonium, while his elder daughter danced so beautifully that Prof. Mathur often cried with joy. He was an adult with the heart of a child. In later years we continued our association, and his family, now much larger, would visit Bombay and stay with us making reunions memorable occasions. They finally moved to Bombay also.

With the help of these two professors we started a College Dramatic Society to stage plays for the benefit of the college library. They along with Prof. Mullamal who was a simple food loving Punjabi scholar, agreed to act if I wrote and directed the plays. In ten days' time, my first play, "The Educated Wife" in Punjabi was ready. It was a hilarious comedy. Prof. Vishnudutt had no difficulty in arranging the funds from Principal Shri. K.L. Bhatia and we started rehearsals in earnest. I not only wrote, directed but also had the main lead of the heroine in the play. On premier night the show was sold out. I was nervous, but I knew this was an opportunity to prove my worth in show business after my recent disappointing Bombay trip. To add realism, on opening night, instead of stuffing cotton in my blouse I used two inflated rubber balloons. I sauntered on the stage as I made my entry, looking stunning, dressed as a female. Everyone thought I looked ravishing and the audience was delighted with our performances, each actor excelling in his role.

In the final act, Prof. Mullamal who played my stepmother, got so carried away by his own performance that he started adding extra lines and unrehearsed actions. He gave me a bear hug to express his (her) affection in the last scene. Now, he too had added props for a more dazzling effect. He had inserted 'Tin Funnels' in his bra, to enhance his figure. When we embraced, his 'Tin Funnels' and my 'Rubber Balloons' did not agree, and there was a loud bang, my assets burst one by one and the audience guessing correctly began to roar with laughter. I did not want to be seen with a flat chest all of a sudden, and signalled that the curtain should be dropped and so the play came to an unplanned, but striking end. The reviews, the audience reaction and the capacity crowd, plus the money earned for the library fund, convinced the Principal to attend the performance. He was so thrilled with the play and my talent as a Writer, Director and an Actor, that he wanted me to meet the city fathers and the town intelligentsia, as now I was a name to be reckoned with. "The deafest man can hear praise" – Walter S. Landor. I gained a crowd of adoring fans but as always, some people, like my mathematics professor, accused me of being a bore and a shallow showman. To further aggravate him I would tell all kinds of funny, made-up stories to impress my listeners. Actually if there was anyone that I was deceiving, it was my own self.

With my scholarship, tuition earnings and with the sale of my paintings, I was managing quite comfortably.

I dressed like a dandy but behaved like a prince. I loved to wear a bow tie and a butterfly collar. Youth is a short lived phase in everyone's life, followed by hot summer, then monsoon and the cold winter of old age. Those were the days when I looked at my face in the mirror and whispered to myself. "Who says I am an ugly duckling? Who?"

With regular morning exercise, I even managed to develop two almond sized muscles on my biceps. I was a clever student in every subject except mathematics, which never interested me. My maths professor, predicted that I would only get 1.5% marks in the University Examination. At last the day came when I had to appear for the University Examination to pass my F.Sc. test, and the first examination was in mathematics. There were 10 questions we had to answer. Dressed in black, I lived up to the nickname awarded me by my fellow students – 'Black Prince.' I entered the examination hall, greeted everybody with a smile and said a polite "Good Morning Sir" to my professor. Soon I took my seat which was right under the nose of the head examiner. The stationery and papers were already spread on the desks and it was written on the black board in bold letters, "If you need extra stationery, just stand up and ask".

Then the big sheets of question papers were distributed among the candidates and all the good students got busy answering the easy questions first. For me there wasn't an easy question. So I too pretended to the absorbed in answering the questions.

I noticed that many of the bright students were asking for graph paper, which was a mystery to me. They were given these sheets. I too wanted to show off, so stood up and asked for the paper with the crisscross lines. I said, "Sir, may I have a sheet or two of that 'rough paper'".

The examiner was amazed and said, "What did you say? Please repeat'.

I repeated what I had said earlier, which caused a muted giggle amongst the students and that infuriated the examiner who said, "It is called a 'Graph Paper' and not 'Rough-Paper'. Don't you know that it is used for making graphs". I apologized and sat down. Now, I did not know math, but I knew that the urge to go to the toilet was inversely proportional to my ability to solve any question. I felt that I must relieve myself so that I could at least sit through this torture comfortably. So, I got up again and held up my trembling hand, but before I could open my mouth, the examiner said. "Yes, now what do you need smart guy?" I replied "Sir, urgent human needs compel me to ask your kind permission to go to the bathroom, as I must…"

Before I could finish he yelled "SIT DOWN! I understand your game."

I obeyed, but my need was most urgent now. So, I got up again and said, "Sir, you may send the peon with me to the bathroom, I cannot control myself any more and the human urge." He again yelled, "Sit down I said." So I sat down, but quickly stood up again. Again he shouted. "Yes?" and I said in a loud voice, "May I have lots of blotting paper, Sir?"

My words made everyone in the hall burst out with laughter, even the examiner could see pain, agony and urgency written on my face. He ordered the peon to accompany me to the washroom with instructions to keep a watch over my every movement. I came back and somehow solved two mathematical problems, on the question paper. In other subjects, I did quite well, but I had a faint suspicion that I would not get through, and would have to waste a year more in my class. After ten days the University exams were over and we had holidays.

▲ My father Pandit. Ralliaram Sharma in his younger days.
To me he was always my best friend.

◀ My father and me,

My mother Dhan Devi with my youngest brother Kesho and my little sister Guro (left)

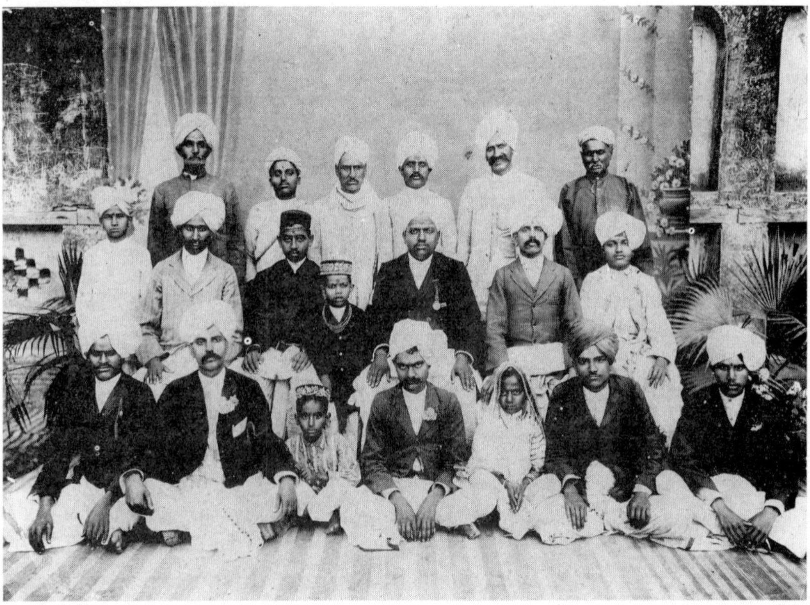

At M/S TORMAL UTTAM CHAND) where my father worked. I am seated beside my dad (bottom row - 2nd and 3rd from left

Our uncle and saviour Pandit Kirparam who came to our aid during our hardest time. He bought me my first camera.

Khalsa College (seated 3rd from left, second row).

My sister Taro died of TB at a very young age. I had to pretend toread the holy Gita to her, because it was her last wish. Then she died peacefully.
"To live in hearts we leave behind is not to die" – Thomas Campbell.

▲

Principal Bhatiaji supported my efforts to raise funds for the college. He is seated 3rd from left, in the middle row, while I am seated on the extreme right.

◀

When I was barely ten years old. Poverty had taught me to fend for myself very early in life. I remember cutting cardboard pieces to place inside my worn out shoes to protect me from the severe Punjab winters.

▼

On the 1st of August in 1927 I matriculated with top honours from the University of the Panjab.

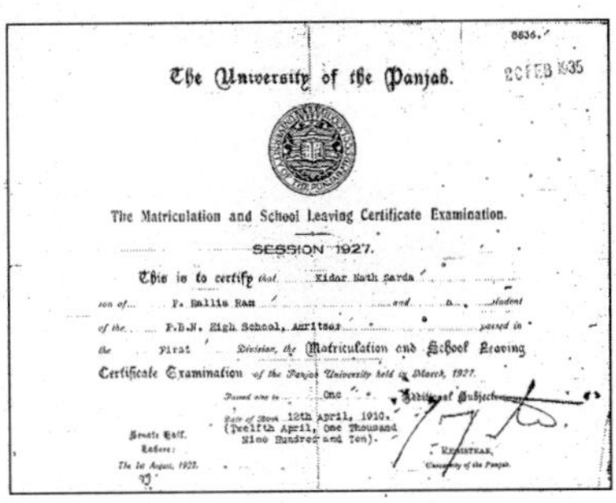

8636.

The University of the Panjab. 20 FEB 1935

The Matriculation and School Leaving Certificate Examination.

SESSION 1927.

This is to certify that Kidar Nath Sarda son of P. Ballia Ram and a student of the P.B.N. High School, Amritsar passed in the First Division, the Matriculation and School Leaving Certificate Examination of the Panjab University held in March, 1927.

Passed also in One Additional Subject.

Date of Birth 12th April, 1910. (Twelfth April, One Thousand Nine Hundred and Ten).

Senate Hall, Lahore: The 1st August, 1927.

Registrar, University of the Panjab.

Some of my teachers were more like friends, in particular my Art teacher Master Gurdit Singh with whom I ran away to Bombay. Others who became good friends were Prof. Mathur and Principal Bhatiaji. That is not to say that I did not have enemies. There were some professors who positively disliked me.

In my first directorial venture, Master Gurdit Singh who played the drunken husband with Miss Anayati They were both so convincing that when he appeared at the premiere of the movie, the audience booed him for being such a nasty man.

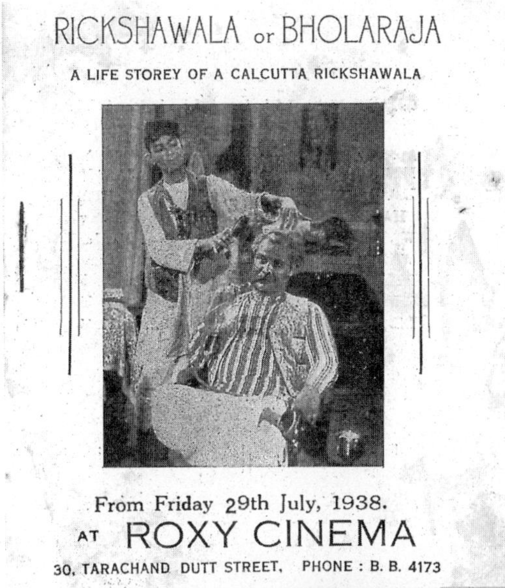

My first assignment for Ranjit Movitone was a story called *Rickshawala*

With Thakur Singh who had asked me to accompany him on his trip, to paint the portraits of royalty.

right: The Maharajah of the Rajwada who ordered his portrait. The King became so enraged when he could not see his other ear in the profile thatThakur Singh had painted, that we ran away from fear of being tossed in prison for life.

A pencil portrait that I did of Pandit Nehru. He liked it so much he asked me to autograph it so he could hang it in his office. I agreed on two conditions. One that he in turn autograph a copy for me which I would always keep in my office, and secondly that he toosign inEnglish, something he rarely ever did at that time.

Chapter 5

"Women are wiser than men because they know less and understand more."

James Stephens

It was during these holidays that something wonderful happened. A chance meeting with Mr. Nandlal, the head of the Temperance Society, gave me my first chance to write and direct a 16 mm short film, depicting the evils of alcohol. I jumped at the opportunity. Now Mr. Nandlal — Babu Nandlal, as he was called, was an old and experienced man of sixty eight, while I was still a young man of eighteen – a gap of half a century, so I was a bit awestruck. Babu Nandlal had seen my performance as the 'Educated Wife', the busty glamourous girl. He liked old cars with big headlights, and also women with big bold bosoms. He was also a connoisseur of dramatic art and a very famous and respected figure. He liked me, respected me, even addressed me as Kidarji. He proposed that if I could write a good script dealing with the evils of drinking, he would make some funds available from Temperance Society to produce a silent film. I agreed.

He pondered for a while, and then ordered two cups of tea and added, "I have four conditions, and if you do not agree to these conditions, I would not be interested in producing the film." His four conditions were. First, — nobody including the cast would ask for a remuneration. This is charitable work and therefore should be voluntary, but if the society feels satisfied, some gifts may be given. Second, — the shooting must be completed in 10 to 12 days. Third – The terrace of Temperance premises should be used as the studio, because there was enough sunlight and reflectors could easily be arranged. And finally, no female actress or any one's relative, could enter the main Temperance Hall where there was a watchman day and night.

I thought it wiser to agree to all the conditions; I could start production, and then if it became necessary, I could always appeal for some consideration. Soon the script was ready and was immediately approved. The hero's role of the drunkard husband was given to Master Gurdit Singh, my companion in our Bombay adventure. Other minor roles were allocated to Babu Nandlal's circle of friends. But I insisted that for the role of the heroine, the suffering wife we should get a real actress and not a boy dressed as one. He said, "It's your headache to find one." But when I reminded him about his last condition he replied with a smile. "Young man those conditions were just for the record — you are the director, do what you want except do not make me a party to your plans. I will never visit the shooting, and will only see the film when it is ready."

So the search for a suitable heroine began. In those days, no girl from a middle class family would perform for an audience – so the option was to recruit from amongst the 'Dancing Girls', who were unlikely to be convincing as the innocent lady for our script.

I was told that there was a B-grade theatrical company, staging some C-class plays in one of the old theatres of Amritsar. I approached their manager, with a request to meet the leading lady but, was told to meet the make-up man Mr. Pyarelal. He took me to his sister, Anayati the leading lady.

Miss Anayati had the innocent face of a schoolgirl, but a large frame. Her voice was soft but the language she used was foul. She used four-letter words without hesitation, and further emphasized them with gestures of her hands and fingers. I tolerated all this for the sake of 'art,' and in the manner of a gentleman I bashfully told her the purpose of my visit. This was the first big break for me as a movie director, and her big chance to star in a movie which would be shown not only in India but perhaps all over the world. Then I narrated the story to her, but also added, "I am just a student and so I can only afford Rs. 101 as a token gift, which I promise to pay on the first day of shooting." I also told her that I would arrange for her conveyance and lunch and the project would only require 5 to 6 shifts from 10.00 am. to 4.00 pm. and that her theatrical performances would not be interrupted. And if she agreed we could start on the following Friday.

Miss Anayati, was very gracious and understanding. She took my hand and shaking it remarked: "*Hazoor mujhe sub manzoor hai.Main zaroor iss film main kaam karungi.*" (Sir, I agree to all your conditions. I definitely want to work in this film). I got up to go, but she said "No Sir, you will have to have a cup of tea with me first before you leave". So Pyarelal was asked to fetch the tea and my heroine got up to comb her hair.

I noticed that Anayati had big, bold breasts which like naughty children wanted to come out and play, but remained under the cover of her thin blouse. She realised I was staring at her and like an animal trainer in the circus, she pushed the naughty twins back inside her translucent blouse. Feeling embarrassed I gulped my tea as fast as I could reminding her I would pick her up on Friday.

On the day of our first shooting, Miss Anayati promptly reported to work. She behaved like a perfect lady never using a filthy word. Everybody was impressed with her performance and her behaviour. We managed to complete the work in four days instead of six. I decided to play a small role of the thief, who gets caught by the heroine's servants. The servants were played by Pyarelal and his associate Babu Master the tailor.

I had directed them that when they caught me they were to pretend to beat me. They nodded. "*Han Hazoor, Han Hazoor*". (Yes, Sir, Yes, Sir).

As soon as I said "Camera" and we started shooting, they both took out *Paans* and started chewing the betel leaf, then they approached me, the thief, and caught me in a powerful grip. They did not hammer me, but rubbed me against the stone wall, again and again with such force that my entire back was bruised. Then to show their contempt they even spat at me. In agony I shouted "Cut". and one of them rushed to get a kitchen knife. I ran from the premises and the cameraman understanding my problem stopped the man. Thank God this was the last shot of the film. For three days I was in bed with an injured back and aching muscles. Realism proves so costly in films!

When I was able to move around, I learned that Miss Anayati and her unit were leaving town, so I rushed to say goodbye. She was very happy to see me and showed me a note she had written in Urdu, with instructions to have it delivered to me. Since Pyarelal had gone out on some urgent work, she begged me to wait with her, as she was feeling awfully lonely. She spoke sadly "We are not going to meet again, never, so let us spend a few moments together Kidar!" Seated by me, she continued, "You may think that my filthy language and behaviour makes me a real bitch, but believe me I was not born bad". Her eyes were moist, and like a little girl, keen to pour her heart out, she held my hand and said, "I hold your hand because I am frightened even of the memory of that awful night."

She paused and then continued, "When I was ten my father died in an accident. We lived in a small town near Sialkot. My mother was very pious and we were very poor. Since we had no place to stay, our Uncle Sultan, who was my father's best friend, offered to help us and took us to Sialkot, where he worked as a night watchman in a girl's school called Mother Mary Christian High School. Uncle Sultan had a wife who was very hot tempered, but he still gave us a small room in his house. Both my mother and I, in turn, served as servants there, and we also worked for two other neighbours to supplement our income. My mother was very religious and serious, while I was outgoing and jovial. I started growing faster than any of the girls my age and by the time I was twelve, I looked like a fifteen year old. I was considered a charming young lady. One day Uncle Sultan gave my mother Rs. 10 and ordered her to go to a neighbouring village by train to fetch his pregnant wife, and told her to bring her back the next afternoon. That night Uncle Sultan asked me to cook his dinner and bring it to him to the school. At about 8:30 I took his meals to the room in the school as instructed. He was lying on a cot groaning with pain. I asked him what the matter was and he said, that as usual, he had an attack of nasty stomach pain. I remembered that whenever he suffered from pain his wife or my mother would rub some oil on his stomach. So, I rushed back home and hurried to get some warm oil. I started to rub the oil on his stomach, but I did not suspect what he was about to do. I had no idea that destiny and the devil in Uncle Sultan had conspired to ruin my innocence…" She stopped and started sobbing, after a while she murmured, "I hope you understand…" I nodded and promised never to tell anyone her tragic story. She continued in a low tone, "When this heinous crime was committed I was horrified, frightened, hurt and humiliated. I was totally dazed because he had tied me to his bed all along. Then he untied me, threw my *shalwar kameez* on my naked body and ordered me to get dressed. Uncle Sultan then took four silver coins from his pocket and placed them in my hand. He said, "Good girl, remember if you tell anyone I will ruin both you and your mother – now go home."

"I walked out in a trance, I was shattered to bits, to tally humiliated. I remember that, a good and trusted friend of mine Pyarelal, had told me that he was going away that evening, and had asked me to see him off at the railway station. He was travelling to Lahore to meet his Uncle, who was a director of a theatrical company, to get a job with him. As I walked back through the deserted school grounds I noticed a small chapel and a light from a burning candle. In it was a statue of Jesus nailed to the cross. I am not a Christian but I felt an affinity with him and began to weep. I noticed a small charity box in the corner. I placed my four coins in the box, whispering, "This is my donation", and left.

"I wandered aimlessly in the street and soon heard the chimes of a clock in the distance, it was 10:00 p.m. I decided not to go home, because I could never face my mother or any one else at home again. I continued walking towards the railway station. I entered a vacant compartment and felt alone and equally empty. The train started with a jolt. Suddenly a hand was placed on my shoulder and a sympathetic voice said "Anayati what are you doing here? Why are you crying?" I looked up to find my friend Pyarelal. I could not look into his eyes and so remained silent. He seemed to understand my plight and said, "*Pagli* (crazy girl), I am your elder brother. What is wrong?"

I slowly confided in him and told him I could never go back home. He then told me that his sister had suffered an identical fate. She had fallen victim to a gang of hoodlums, who raped her and left her abandoned in a sugarcane field. I stopped sobbing and Pyarelal pledged that he would protect me as his sister and brought me to Lahore with him. I too got a job with the theatrical company, and till today he protects me and continues to treat me like his sister."

I sat there in silence, stunned. Shortly after she stopped narrating her tale the sound of footsteps seemed to break the dead silence that had fallen. She got up wiped the tears from her eyes, and after composing herself said, "*Khuda Hafiz* (may God be your protector), Kidarji, we part never to meet again… I want to thank you for treating me with respect."

As she walked away, I stood there in total awe and respect for the lady who, at our first meeting, had come across as a foul mouthed, uncouth woman.

When everyone at the Temperance hall saw the film they were full of praise. However that was not so when it was shown to the public for the first time when the main star Master Gurdit Singh was present. After the screening the public spotted him, started abusing him, calling him a dog and a brute. He had given such a convincing performance that they thought that he was truly like the character in the film, and that the story they had seen, was real. I was happy with the outcome, but deep inside I knew my work was amateurish. I needed training before could I venture to make another movie.

Babu Nandlal and the members of the Temperance Society rewarded me, and gave me an envelope with a letter of appreciation. The envelope contained Rs. 601. The letter explained that the Rs 101 was reimbursement for my payment to Anayati and the balance was for me. With Rs. 601, I managed to enrol myself in Khalsa College in Amritsar. I also managed to buy a second hand bicycle since the college was about 5 miles from where I stayed. The bicycle was a bargain since it cost me only five rupees.

The journey to and from college was long and monotonous. One day as I followed a *tanga* (horse and buggy) I noticed a beautiful girl in the open seat at the back of the vehicle. She was facing me as I rode behind. Every time the tanga went over a bump or a rock, her head would jerk up and down as if she was nodding and beckoning to me. So I started nodding from side to side in response to her jerking up and down nods, suggesting no-no I can't. Soon it seemed we were synchronized and in perfect rhythm. She moving her head up and down and me nodding from side to side. Those who noticed, laughed and laughed.

I completed my B. Sc. in the next two years. My father insisted I should complete my masters degree. He once again arranged some money for me to continue my studies at Khalsa College. I had chosen English as my main subject, and Professor T.H. Advani was very happy because I was his favourite student. He quoted, "The primary purpose of education is not to teach you to earn your bread, but to make every mouthful of words sweeter." – James R, Angell

I was enamoured by theatre, and men like Aga Hashar Kashmiri. For the opening lines of a play about a prostitute and her audience, he wrote, *"Mridang kahe, dhhrig hai, Dhhrig hai, sitaar kahe kin ko, kin ko? Doo haath utha kur naar kahey, inn ko, inn ko, inn ko, inn ko."* There are few examples of better symphonic alliteration. I joined a theatrical unit started by some amateur actors in Amritsar. Here I met Mr. A.S. Gyani, who nine years later, in 1940, was to play the role of Kumar Giri, in my biggest box office hit movie, now considered an all time classic 'Chitralekha'. Mr. Gyani was a dentist who loved acting.

Though I was admitted to this theatrical group, I was not considered fit to act; my looks, my voice and my build being the main obstacles. I was however allowed to watch them rehearse every night from 9 p.m. to 1:30 a.m. My father who understood my love for the profession allowed me to attend those rehearsals. I was dazzled by Mr. Gyani's performance and whenever he needed a glass of water I would run to fetch it for him. I thought that every time I touched his hand, some of his skill and knowledge would be transferred to me like an electric current. I made sure I always touched his hand each time I offered him a glass of water. Mr. Gyani ignored me, and never knew in what high regard I held him.

Since they bypassed me and never offered me a role, or any other involvement, a friend of mine and I decided to start our own Theatrical Company. We needed a thousand rupees. So we agreed that each of us would contribute half the amount. I discussed this with my father but he said that he could only manage Rs. 250. I scraped together the balance. Actors from the previous group who, like me, were ignored, were quick to join our group. With the help of my father, who knew some old actors of a Parsi Stage company from Bombay and Calcutta, we hired Master B.O. who was then unemployed and glad to get a job. Master B.O. had a commanding personality and a thundering voice. He was also once a big star. We selected a play called 'Shrimati Manjari'. I did not get a role, but since I was one of the financiers I was happy to be involved.

Here I met Mahinder Singh, our production manager. He was the son of an advocate in Amritsar and proved to be very helpful and valuable with his father's influence. At last the play was ready. We booked the biggest theatre in Amritsar called Mahn Singh Theater. The Director gave his last minute instructions to Mahinder, who turned out to be a show off, always trying to impress us with his father's status and connections.

The director said. "I need a velvet seat." To which Mahinder immediately replied, in his usual style, "Don't worry I will pinch my father's."

Master B.O. then said. "We also need two large balls for the cannon scene." Mahinder replied. "Don't worry I will pinch my father's, he has two paper weights that were presented to him by a Japanese monk."

Master B.O. continued, "And for the third act we need a grave."

To which Mahinder immediately replied: "Don't worry I will bring my father's."

When every body began to laugh he realized his mistake. He did however get his father's suitcase which we covered with a sheet to look like a *mazaar*.

I quickly learned that show business has its problems, its headaches and heart aches. On opening night we had managed to get a full house and had reserved about 80 seats for our own staff and other prominent and important officials. Our hero Mr. Hameed Mukhtar requested 41 complementary seats. He wanted 40 in the first row and one in the second row. To which Mahinder said. "Have you invited Ali Baba and the 40 thieves?" This upset our hero, and to take revenge he distributed ten seats in the first row to his henchmen to disturb the show on the opening night, and refused to act at the very last minute. The director got wind of this and was very upset. I learned about this half an hour before the play was to commence. We were all stunned and in a state of panic. My partner and I tried to reason with our hero Mukhtar, but he was adamant and refused to reconsider. But as the old saying goes — "The Show Must Go On".

A gentleman named Pundit Kirpa Ram, who was an advocate, had attended some of the rehearsals. He offered to help. He said he needed at least twenty minutes between each act to study the lines, and with the proper prompting, he would act the main role. Twenty minutes is like an eternity to an impatient audience, so I was told to go on stage and hold the attention of the audience until Pundit Kirparam could study his lines and his moves.

The play was in three Acts, which meant that I was to provide entertainment to the audience and to clown about for two intermissions of twenty minutes each. It was an ordeal to not only select a performing partner, but to think of a skit on the spot under the pressure.

Acting was thrust on me that fateful night. I went behind the stage and whispered, "*Nath to nay ghaj ke Bandh*", the *Bhajan* my grandmother had taught me to get divine help. The play started, Pundit Kirparam performed with such charm and gusto, that the audience watched it in pin drop silence, and then clapped enthusiastically for several minutes. The deserter Ahmed

Mukhtar, was there in the front row, with his henchmen, ready with rotten eggs and tomatoes for any actor who faltered, or failed to deliver his lines on stage. But the eager and appreciative audience prevented him from causing any trouble,

The intermission after Act 1 allowed the audience to go out, and during this gap I called Master Gurdit Singh and my friend Bhagat Singh to brief them about the short skit we were to perform on stage as comics, to allow Pundit Kirparam to prepare for his next act.

As the audience reassembled, I was pushed on the stage. My funny voice, my odd features and my skinny frame added to the credibility of the 'Pitiable Servant' character I was to play on stage, and I was loved by the crowd. They roared with laughter watching my funny gestures and enjoyed my squeaky voice. Being a poet, I even added some humorous couplets and won the hearts of the appreciative crowd. The main play was a great success. Pundit Kirparam proved himself a real star and Kidar Nath was an overnight sensation.

Excited and exhilarated I returned home without removing the grease-paint from my face. All the dogs in the area greeted me by barking and following me.

I thought this was some reception — like a hero's welcome. Soon they started growling and I discovered their real intention, and I felt that I was under organized attack. I ran for my life with the dogs in hot pursuit. Who says that 'barking dogs seldom bite'. Thanks to my baggy pants, the fashion in those days, my legs were protected, and ensured that the dogs did not get a sample of my flesh. Hearing all the noise, my father and the neighbourhood woke up and they rescued me from these dirty dogs. My pants were ripped to shreds and portions of my jacket were missing.

Next day the Urdu papers praised the skinny squeaking clown in the short skits. My name was not mentioned since no one knew who I was. By public demand the play had to be staged three more times. Now my name was added to all the publicity material in bold letters. We made a net profit of eight thousand rupees. Thus ended 1931 on a happy note. 1932 had more surprises in store for me.

Chapter 6

"Life has taught us that love does not consist in gazing at each other, but in looking together in the same direction."

Antoine de Saint Exupery

In the month of February 1932, my marriage was arranged. My father-in-law was rich and well placed. He insisted that the *baraat* (marriage party) should travel from Amritsar to Bannu, a town far up near the North West Frontier Province. This not only meant extra travel expense, but it also reduced the number of people in the wedding party; people who had initially volunteered, now declined to travel that far. My father was hurt by the excuses made by friends and relatives, who had declined to accompany us at the eleventh hour. Annoyed at this he told my mother, "Don't worry. If I have to travel with only my three sons, Kidar and his two younger brothers, Himmat and Kesho, I will do so and bring home our *Bahu* (Daughter-in-law)."

As is the custom, I was to ride on the back of a decorated white horse, along with a small boy, also dressed in white, who sat behind me. I wore the traditional Achkan or a long coat, churidar pajama or tights and a pink turban with a *mukat* (crown) and *kasuri jutta*, (thin narrow shoes). The strings of flowers draped from my turban, which flowed in front of my face, made it difficult for me to see clearly what was happening. Around me women were singing as they gathered to join the procession. My sister was busy with prayers. I, with a sword in hand was thrilled and excited. My two brothers danced madly on the street. The band was playing, everything was going smoothly when suddenly a dust storm darkened the sky. The menacing storm accompanied by howling winds ripped through the marching procession. Soon trees were uprooted, electric poles came crashing down, glass windows shattered.

In utter panic everyone ran for shelter. My father helped my mother and the children to find cover. The singing ladies had dispersed. A short-circuit now plunged the area in total darkness. Even the attendant of the horse, the *Saies* deserted me. There was a sudden flash of lightning followed by louder crashes of thunder. There I sat on the horse in the middle of the street, with my little companion who had now started crying, and clung to me in utter fright. Suddenly there was an even louder clap of thunder.

The horse could take it no more and started galloping at full speed down the road. In my right hand I held the sword and with my left I grabbed on to the horse's mane, as best as I could, with the frightened child clinging on to me for life. My father ran after me shouting, "Help, Help", but we had shot right past everyone. I am no horse rider and I wonder how I managed to stay on the saddle as the horse surmounted all obstacles and hurdles. If he had been in a steeplechase, I am sure he would have won any race my right hand still clinging to the sword, and my left still gripped on to the mane. The flowers around my head flowing in all directions now gave me a clear vision of my impending doom. Suddenly, the little sobbing boy clutching on to me, in utter panic and urinated. A warm fluid soaked the saddle and overflowed down my pajamas into my golden shoes. I thought it was a great test and a challenge to be a bridegroom. As soon as the horse arrived under the porch of the *Kotwaali* or police station the horse thought he was safe, and stopped as suddenly as he had started the race. I was still in the saddle with the little fellow crying and clinging to me like a leech, he once again started urinating.

The philosopher in me, reminded me that on the day I was born there was a big storm, and now on the day I was to be married the storm was keeping me company. Maybe I am a 'Child Of The Storms'. And I predict that the day I die there will also be a fierce storm to scare off my faithful friends who will come to attend my funeral procession.

Suddenly I noticed my father running and panting to reach me. When he got closer he thanked his stars to find both of us in one piece. He picked up the little fellow and set him on the ground, then he unburdened me of my sword, and asked me to dismount from the runaway horse. Suddenly he noticed my pajamas dripping with fluid and he began to laugh. "So Kidar Nath?" As if to imply that I was shit scared of getting married. I hurriedly replied, "It was he", pointing to the little boy.

There was a lull after the storm. After reaching the station, and a two day journey by train the marriage party reached Bannu. The local priest placed me on a *Kharra*, a woven seat, and a burning lamp was placed under me. The heat almost roasted my bottom. I jumped up when the ordeal by fire became unbearable. After this Raj Dulari, my beautiful bride, and I were married. I brought home the shy bride. She proved to be all the strength, inspiration and support I would need in life. She had studied at the best women's institute, and had reached high levels of Sanskrit. Since my grounding was basically Urdu, wherever I have used Hindi in my films with sensitivity, it has been all her influence.

Six weeks later, I was to appear for my M.A. examination and had to go to Lahore for that exam. After the examination my father suggested that I take my wife to a nearby hill station for our honeymoon. This immediately resulted in an indignant comment from my mother who said, "When I was married, why wasn't I taken to a hill station? Why?" A robust argument ensued and the trip was aborted.

In the evening, I met Sardar Thakur Singh, the renowned painter from Punjab. He asked me to travel to some Native States or Rajwadas with him as his P.R.O. for about three weeks, all expenses paid and an additional fee of Rs. 500 would be given to me. I agreed, as S. Thakur Singh was a thorough gentleman, a very simple soul, who had never gone to school, or taken tuitions, but was very fond of speaking 'English' on every possible occasion, whenever there was a chance to express his intention, sentiments or commands.

His English was not King's English, as is generally known, but his own special brand of 'Made in Punjab' English.

Once, in order to impress me, he said, "Worry not, Mr. Kidar Nath, I am like your enlarged brother." (He meant big brother). And then he continued, "I shall always be looking behind you!" (He meant "looking after you") He then added, "If, when you pass M.A. and you don't get no job, I shall, offer you a good job, come to Calcutta, and fill the vacancy beneath me in Madan Theaters". He worked as the Chief Scene Painter in Madan Theatres in Calcutta.

He had plans to visit some Rajwadas or Native States of those days, to get some royal assignments and make a fortune. He needed me badly, because I was well read and could express in English, the "Artist's (S. Thakar Singh), dreams on canvas, in oil colours."

He showed me his latest painting of a bathing beauty, a gorgeous girl in a wet sari standing at the *Ghat* (river bank). And I exclaimed, "Oh dear, what a pair!" Thakur Singh was a bit surprised and said, "Pair? I only painted my wife, whom I use as my model, in a wet sari on the Ganga Ghat. She has no companion!" My prompt reply was, "What about the reflection in the clear water, Sardarji?" He then nodded with pride, and I thanked God that the situation was salvaged. What I had actually meant earlier you yourself can guess.

We visited Udaipur and were a great success there. The main reason was that the then Maharaja of Udaipur was a great intellectual who had an appreciative eye for a good piece of art. Then we were recommended to go to some remote Rajwada on the border of Rajasthan and Gujarat, where no artist had ever gone, and where there was good money for an artist like Sardar Thakur Singh. So we carried along some select paintings and the newly acquired Certificates of Recommendations from the Maharaja of Udaipur.

We reached our destination at night, and were cordially received at a small railway station, some five miles away from the Rajwada. We were lodged in the Royal Guest House, with one Popatlal as our special attendant to look after our needs, translate the local language into simple Hindi for us, and get us exchange for our British Money (Kaldar), since the Rajwada used its own currency. He was our friend, philosopher and guide.

The next day, we were told to take a day's rest as His Highness had gone hunting with his noblemen. At night, when I returned to our room, I was amazed to see Sardarji practising some Kathak steps, standing in front of a big mirror. When I questioned his funny act, and his *Ta Thai Tat Thai*, he replied, "Popatlal has told me that tomorrow morning, I shall be taken to the Darbar for *Mujra* and I know nothing about dancing!" Poor Sardarji, he did not know that *Mujra* meant bowing low before His Highness, when he was presented in the Royal Darbar. He knew *Mujra* in Punjabi meant the steps of a Dancing Girl. When I explained this to him, he relaxed and thanked me for my timely help and my general knowledge.

Next day, Sardarji was taken to the royal court and was commissioned to paint a big portrait of His Highness. Sardar Thakur Singh was very impressed by the shapely nose of His

Highness, and it took him three days, a one hour sitting on each day, to complete the portrait — 'The Profile Of The Majestic Maharaja'. On the fourth day, he brought the canvas to the Guest House to add some highlights here and there, and to make the pearls and silken tassels look real. He was a Master of painting silk and golden ornaments set with precious stones.

The profile of His Highness was stunning, and we both expected a big reward for this superb piece of work. As Popatlal was on leave the next day, another attendant arranged for our conveyance to the royal court. We entered with high hopes of being praised. The Darbar Hall was packed with Royal guests and noblemen. His Royal Highness was expecting a masterpiece from the renowned artist Sardar Thakur Singh. I had covered the painting with a silken scarf, and had followed Thakur Singh as he sauntered ahead with a big smile on his face, which even his big beard could not hide. We both bowed as low as we could. Then like a magician I unveiled the show piece saying, "Here it is Sir, the great profile by the great artist Sardar Thakur Singh." We eagerly awaited some applause and acclamation, similar to what we had experienced in Udaipur. We were shocked when everyone jumped to their feet, the moment His Highness sprang up as if he had received an electric shock. There was a moment of silence and to break the ice Thakur Singh politely asked, "Your Highness, how do you like your portrait? So unusual — as you are facing left, the left side is the best side of your profile." His Highness was furious and yelled. "For God's sake correct it, take it back how dare you call it my portrait. Where is my right ear... and and the rare ruby on that right ear… take it back and bring it back on Monday, and make sure you also include my other eye along with my other ear. Oh ! why have you made a caricature of me… why?…why?" And with these words he stormed out of the hall in a huff, and all his entourage followed him to the royal palace, downcast as if in mourning.

The kindly attendant came to us and said, "You'd better disappear as soon as possible. Forget about Monday and his royal portrait. Once His Highness loses his temper anything can happen and you don't want to upset him again. There are offenders in jail for smaller crimes, for the last 30 years. I was a young boy when a singer from Banaras offended His Highness and only yesterday did the poor singer finally get his freedom." I asked, "Was the singer finally released?" "No", replied the attendant, "he died yesterday and so there is a vacancy in the prison to be filled."

This made Thakur Singh shiver with fear; we quickly wrapped the portrait back in the silken scarf, and took to our heels. We decided it would be best to leave town as quickly as possible before His Highness decides to order his police force to keep an eye on us. Popatlal, who had not witnessed the incident arrived. We told him that the painting was liked and then handed him a hundred rupees as *bakshish* (a tip); we also gave him some money for our return tickets back to Amritsar along with our luggage. We added that we were going sightseeing and that we would reach the station soon. Popatlal was happy with the reward and advised us that the next train was scheduled to leave in three hours, so we should reach there by that time.

In terror of being recognized, we decided to walk incognito to the railway station, which was about five miles away. We decided that we would leave as two *sadhus* (monks), a guru and his *chaila* (disciple), to avoid being recognized. But we had no saffron attire, traditionally worn by the religious men in India. So Sardarji suggested that we wrap a *longati* (loin cloth), and smear our bodies with ashes. We went up the terrace of the guest house and made a small bonfire of the Royal portrait and our clothes. We tore up Sardarji's yellow turban to make two *langoties* and smeared our bodies with the ashes, mixed with some talcum powder and the oil paint we had brought along. Then Thakur Singh untied his beard and his long hair. He looked like a real sadhu with his wild flowing hair and beard. The smoke had made his eyes turn red which made him look more real.

We escaped through the back door of the Royal Guest House and took the lonely road to the station. On the way, we encountered a few farmers and some old ladies who immediately stopped and raised their hands in prayer and for blessing at the sight of the two pious men. We nodded and walked faster. No one suspected our camouflage except for a few cows who ran away when they saw us.

Popatlal on reaching the station had already bought our tickets, and placed our luggage in the first class compartment, and since he had to wait there for us, and he had a hundred rupees in his pocket, could not resist having a few glasses of *Tharra* (country wine). He was soon tipsy and whistled merrily as he waited for us near the door of the compartment. As we reached the deserted Railway Station the train began to move slowly. We ran towards Popatlal, jumped in, and somehow got him off the train. He fell in a ditch but he was too drunk to notice what had happened. But he did hurl abuse at the two holy men who had dumped him. The train slowly pulled out of the Rajwada.

We swore never to visit any Rajwada again. We removed the make-up, washed ourselves and got into a new set of clothes from our suitcases. Sardarji wanted to celebrate our narrow escape, and so he took out a bottle of whisky from his suitcase and had a few pegs, while I, the teetotaller, was glad we were safe and had enjoyed the adventure. I told Thakur Singh to forget about Rs 500 he had promised to pay me. This made him happier; he sang all the way home. After a thirty-six hours journey we returned home to Amritsar. My family was surprised to see us back so soon, but when we narrated our adventure they were glad to see us back alive, and we all celebrated.

Chapter 7

"The value of a sentiment is the amount of sacrifice you are prepared to make for it."

John Galsworthy

Silent movies had just been transformed, and 'Alamara' was the first talkie made in Bombay. Madan Theatres of Calcutta started filming all the popular stage plays, with Miss Kajan, the big star at that time. Miss Kajan was a tall, thin and charming woman with big brown eyes, long hair and her diction was flawless. She was the hot favourite at that time.

In Bombay, Seth Chandulal Shah, was also making talkies like *Radha Rani*, with lilting music and Miss Gauharbai, a versatile artist of the Theater who was the star in the movies made by Ranjit Studios. Cinema was gaining immense popularity and for only four annas the common man could be transported into a make believe world for a couple of hours. As I said earlier, being thin nimble and the lightest, I could still take off my shirt, as my friends carried me over the crowd, thronged around the box office ticket counter, and shoving my hand in the sea of hands through the bars of the window, I always managed to buy tickets for my friends and myself. The bruises I received, as a result, were worth the thrill of the movies, the songs, the lovely music, and the beautiful leading ladies. I also loved pretty faces.

I was enamoured by show business. I preferred the movies made by Seth Chandulal Shah of Ranjit Studio compared to Madan Theatres of Calcutta, who simply bad adaptations of theatrical plays.

But one film from New Theatres of Calcutta was so fascinating and inspiring, that I made up my mind that I had to go to the tinsel town. I felt like a moth being drawn to a burning flame. The name of this movie was Puran Bhagat and the director of the movie was Shri. D.K. Bose. In my opinion he is the greatest movie maker. No one even today can match his subtlety and the mastery of his creative directorial skill. I believe that he was the *Dronachariya* (supreme guru) of film-making and that all subsequent directors have learned a thing or two from him. He was the first director, who experimented with background music and the first who ensured that when a song started, the story did not come to a grinding halt.

His songs like, "*Kya Kaaran Hai Ab Rone Ka, and Javo Javo Aye Mere Saadhu Raho Guru Kay Sangh*", are great examples to prove this. He expressed ideas through symbolism. In *Puran Bhagat,* the hero spoke volumes with his silence, unlike famous actors who wear you down with their rhetoric and gestures, like the great Sohrab Modi, Prithviraj Kapoor or even Chander Mohan who were very theatrical. I saw *Puran Bhagat* several times, alone, and not in the company of my noisy friends. I decided that my goal and my destiny was Show Business, and my Guru the great Debaki Kumar Bose.

My father had dreams of me being a professor or a principal in a college. So one night when he talked again about his plans for me to complete my Ph.D., I shattered all his dreams by saying, "No sir, I will join the films and I shall be a great dream merchant, a great director like Mr. D. K. Bose and that is my final decision, whether I pass or fail my M.A. My destiny is in a film studio, not in any college or institution."

This annoyed my father, amazed my mother and shocked my family and my friends. My father was furious and he used words, gestures and some blows too on the wall, to express his anger and fury. When words of wisdom failed to dissuade me from my path, to leave and travel to Calcutta, my father threatened to disown me, but I was adamant. Then he said in a sad tone. 'Must my own son Kidar Nath, bring a bad name to our family? Must a respectable Brahmin, like me tolerate the insult of having a son, with such high education, join the profession of the *bhands* and mix with pimps and prostitutes?" My wife who was listening, seated in a corner, could not bear to hear any more, and quietly walked away.

My father then tried to plead and reason with me like a good friend saying, "Have you ever seen your face in the mirror? Are you aware of your squeaky voice, poor health, funny build, and your average looks? You are least suited for the film world, films are for well built actors like Prithviraj." And my reply was. "I will prove my worth somehow, some day, please try to understand me – I am hungry." I said getting up. A sad and silent mother served me my meals – I had hurt the entire family with my decision. Cinema was not respectable in those days.

Next day, my father said sarcastically, "So when do you plan to leave for Calcutta?" I told him I was trying to collect some money to buy the cheapest ticket to Calcutta, and some cash for my survival there. I was short of funds and needed Rs. 25 for the railway ticket. As soon as I could earn or raise the money, I would leave immediately. Then his last threat was, "You have to sign a paper disowning you from all my property". I readily agreed, not being interested in ancestral property.

At once he produced a blank sheet of paper and I signed it, with a smile. Then he said sarcastically. "Please try to leave as soon as possible". I retorted, "This time I will certainly obey you." We both stared at each other but no one spoke. Before life lets you look at any of her bounties, what she asks of you is courage.

That night I stayed awake wondering how I could get the loan, when suddenly my young wife placed Rs. 25 in front of me and whispered, "This is all I have, please accept it and go in search of your goal and dreams. I am a helpless woman but a devoted wife." That was Raj Dulari, she made me what I am, she was a great lady. I told her that I was grateful to her and would never be able to repay her debt... Never in all my life. She said nothing more, but there was a tear in her eyes. We were both silent and then she walked away to the kitchen. I could not take my eyes off her as she walked away. My wife was so understanding.

Soon my mother entered to express her pent up feelings. She said that she had not come to stop me from my mission nor to make me promise something on paper, nor did she feel that she was educated enough to argue with me. But she wanted me to listen to what she had to say. She held my trembling hand as I said, "I promise to obey you, whatever you say." There was a long silence, then she said. "You may join the films, but promise me that you won't touch a drop of liquor, you will remain a vegetarian, and finally I do not want you to ever make a movie which is not fit to be seen in the company of a mother and her daughter." Then she kissed my forehead as if blessing me, and without waiting for a "No" or "Yes" from me, just walked away.

It was a Tuesday, when I packed all my fancy clothes in a suitcase to leave Amritsar. I would have felt very lonely had I not had my hopes and dreams to accompany me on the long journey. No one in the family said much as I departed, no words of sympathy or support, no great show of emotions.

I reached the railway station and bought a third class ticket. No one had come to see me off, not even my friend Master Gurdit Singh, who had once accompanied me to Bombay to help me fulfil my dream. I felt very sorry for myself and then I thought to myself, "Who knows, if those I have left behind are more heartbroken than me, who knows if they are more morose tonight, who knows if anyone will even want to eat their dinner tonight in sorrow." I felt that I had been very selfish and had betrayed my father's trust. My father had regarded me as his best friend, and believing in his principles, had stood firm like a rock. It was about 10 pm.

when the train finally pulled out of Amritsar. I spread my bedding on the upper berth and as I lay down, stared at the ceiling above. Thoughts of doubt crossed my mind for the first time — "What if you fail again, like it happened in Bombay. What if you are defeated again and have to go back to where you belong?" Silently I began to sob. The train had now picked up speed and the rhythmic rocking of the train brought back childhood memories of my grandmother who used to put me to sleep; her lullaby reverberating in my ears. Soon I was fast asleep as I dreamt of my grandmother and the *Bhajan* (hymn) she had taught me, to use in my hour of need, reverberated in my ears.

The journey lasted for two days and finally I reached Howrah Station in Calcutta. Strange faces speaking in a totally foreign language surrounded me. Except for the occasional word in English, I heard no Hindi, Urdu, or Punjabi. People seemed to be rushing to get somewhere in a hurry as they pushed and jostled me. I came out of the station carrying my baggage. I decided to take a 'Victoria' to take me to a *Dharamshala* in the Marwari locality known as Bara Bazaar. I was amused to find that the horses that pulled the buggy were barely bigger than goats back home.

I noticed that the Bengali women though not tall, had large eyes and a charm of their own. They wore no blouse but only draped their sari in such a way as to cover their torso, and were very shy and bashful. Reaching the *Dharamshala*, I locked my luggage in the box allocated to me. Next morning I decided to visit my friend, the well known painter Sardar Thakur Singh, with whom I had shared the

Rajwada adventure, and we had escaped as sadhus from Navajo. I travelled by tramcar to Tollygung and located S. Thakur Singh in the compound of Madan Theatre studios.

He was thrilled and surprised to see me. I told him about my plans and my mission and asked him if he would let me sleep in the verandah of his flat at Dharamtulla. He said under certain conditions, namely, "You can only be there in the night and come at 9 pm. and you must leave the premises by 9 a.m. You may not share our premises and you must use the common tap and lavatory located on the ground floor. You may not sing or whistle while you are in my place, and you may not bring visitors. I am sorry those are my conditions, my second wife is very religious and a staunch Sikh. I am different from what you knew me earlier, for her sake these are my demands. Now, if you agree you may come back on Sunday, when I shall be at home the whole day." I had to agree, since I could not afford to stay anywhere else. I said, "Yes Sardarji, thank you for being my big brother."

Every day I would dress up in my finest clothes, like a dandy, and try to gain access to the New Theaters Studio, but I was always refused entry. Then I would walk around the city restricting myself to one meal a day, as my money was running out, spend the evening in a park till 9 pm. before heading back to Thakur Singh's house. Life was hard but I did not feel defeated or miserable. "Even his griefs are a joy long after to one that remembers all that he wrought and endured." – Homer.

I was confident that it was just a matter of time before I would, one day, become a dream merchant, just like D.K.

Bose. So well did I accept my misery that I even wrote a piece wherein man is told, *"Sukh aagar sukh he rahey toe bhi tu ghabbra jaye, aish ghun bunkay teri lazzatoon ko kha jaye."* (If happiness keeps persisting, that itself will terrify you, Indulgence, like a termite will eat away your satisfactions.)

One day I learned that Madan Theatres needed an assistant painter. I needed a job since I was running short of cash. Thakur Singh instructed me to meet a Parsi gentleman called Dinsha Irani, who was the head of the department. Next day I went to see Mr Dinsha Irani, who was also known as Dinsha Baba. I told him that I had come to apply for the Assistant Painter's job and that I was a good painter. But there was another candidate who was also waiting, to apply for the same job. He was a Muslim by the name of Mr. Aslam, and was dressed in a kurta pajama, while I had arrived in a three piece suit and a bow tie with a butterfly collar.

Dinsha Baba was a character — he was short but tough, with naughty eyes a pleasant disposition, a subtle sense of humour, and a very noble heart. Even though outwardly he acted commanding and cruel, he left a permanent impression on me, and I can never forget him. He told us both that the job was temporary, for only two or three months. When we both agreed to accept it, he continued with a mischievous smile. "Good, I will now ask both of you a few questions and I want straight honest answers." There was a short silence and then he continued looking straight at me with his piercing eyes. "First, are you willing to take this job?" "Yes Sir, I am willing", I replied. The he said. "Good, now are you a vegetarian or a non-vegetarian?" I told him that I was a strict vegetarian. Then he turned to Mr Aslam and said, "And you must be a pucca non-vegetarian." Mr Aslam nodded shyly. Then turning back to me he asked me. "Mr. Sharma, do you drink, I mean do you take *daru* or are you a teetotaler?" I replied quite proudly, "Sir, I, Kidar Sharma have never ever touched a drop of liquor in all my life." Dinsha Baba nodded and said, "I thought so", and then quickly turned to Mr Aslam who cast his eyes down for a moment and then replied, "Sir, I have drunk *daru* once in a while to help me forget my misery, my poverty, and my loneliness." This amused Dinsha Baba who muttered, "Loneliness?" "Yes," Aslam continued, "with one glass, single appears double, and with two glasses I become happy and can sing, but with three glasses the whole world seems drunk and I become sober, after all I am not the only silly goat in this world of fools." Dinsha Baba patted him and said, "You are very honest." Then he turned to me and asked, "Mr. Sharma, would you visit the red light area, perhaps in a month or a year, after all you are young, energetic and alone." To which I shot back, "Sir, I will never visit the place of prostitution, it's a stinking flesh market." I continued, producing a character certificate from my College Principle. "Sir, I am a happily married man, with an exemplary moral character, however my vice is humor, my sense of humor does for me what *daru* does for Mr. Aslam. Humor heals all my wounds, it helps me sleep and awaken and revitalizes me, ready to fight my battles another day."

Dinsha Baba turned to Aslam. "What about you?" Aslam replied. "I admit I do visit Sona-Gachi (the red light area of Calcutta) once in a while, it costs me three rupees which means I have to forgo three meals, but after all I do need this vice because I am no angel." Then Dinsha Baba smiled and said, "I am very pleased with both of you, you have both been honest and candid; you will be pleased to know that I will hire both of you. Mr. Sharma will be paid Rs. 100 a month." I was overjoyed and thanked him profusely for his kindness. Then he turned to Aslam and said to him. "Mr. Aslam, you will receive Rs 200 a month, I am sorry that's the best that my budget permits."

I was outraged by his unfairness and protested. "Why? why am I offered less?"

Dinsha Baba's hawk eyes lit up and he said. "Look you are a vegetarian, a teetotaler and a good boy of high morals, but Mr. Aslam's needs are greater, he is not a saint, and his requirements are more expensive — that's why" "

I was stunned by his logic and wanted to protest again, but the phone rang and Dinsha Baba left. Then Aslam turned to me and said,

"Please, Mr. Sharma don't refuse the offer, Mr. Dinsha may sound crazy to you but I promise that I will give you Rs 50 every month so we will both be earning the same amount, and after all this job is only for a couple of months."

It was then that I realized the greatness of both these gentlemen, and here was I showing off about my upright character and my high moral standards.

Dinsha Baba soon returned and asked us to report to work on the 15th of the month, giving us a small payment by way of advance before we left. Each day I had to walk for three hours to get to the Madan Theatres Studio and it took me the same amount of time to get back from my place at Dharamtulla. This way I saved money and now could afford to eat two meals. After a fortnight of employment one night I got very sick with a very high fever. I was thirsty so I got up and wanted to go to the kitchen to get a glass of water, however this meant that I would have to go through the area where Thakur Singh and his family slept. I could not, for fear of breaking my promise, but I was burning and shivering with a temperature. Finally, in the dead of night, I decided to go to the municipal taps. When I reached the tap it was dry. I walked back and waited for dawn, when I knew Thakur Singh's wife woke up to say her prayers. A persian couplet applies appropriately, *"Uz baalon purr ghubaar-e-tumanna fashanda em, burr shakh-e-gul gira na bawad aashianay ma."* (The bird dusts off the weight of desires from its feathers, lest the rose branch, where she is nesting, snaps under the load).

Thakur Singh had two wives Bayant Kaur or Banti his first wife, and a much younger one. His reason for marrying again was that Banti could not bear him any children. I spent an agonizing night and at dawn Banti came to me and said, "Are you sick, I could hear your muffled groans all night?" I told her that indeed I had a high fever. She ran back into the house and fetched two glasses of water and placing one near me said, "You should have knocked on the door and told Thakur Singh about your fever." She did not perform her puja (prayers) that day, she sat near me and said, "Let me prepare some food for you and for the rest of the family." I asked her not to bother, and not to take any extra trouble for me. At which point she said, "Look I have no relatives, and no children, so if I treat you as my younger brother where is the harm? It would only make me happy."

In the afternoon she took me to her family doctor, who advised complete rest for a week. And my newly acquired elder sister told the doctor that she would look after me. On the way back she asked me, "Why don't you receive any letters from home?" I told her that I had not informed them about my whereabouts. She was thoughtful for a moment and then said. "Will you believe that I have never received a letter all my life, the reason is simple. I have no one to write to me." Then she was sad, silent and after a long pause said, "Anyway when you achieve your goal, and become a famous film director, will you please write a postcard to me so I can treasure it all my life. Please write exactly what I say so that when I receive the postcard, I don't have to ask anyone to read the precious communication to me, O.K? Now write as follows: My Dear Sister Banti Kaur, you are a kind, loving and religious person. Then why has Destiny planned a life for you which is trying, troublesome, treacherous and torturous? May death snatch you soon from this ugly life, and free you from all your agony." Her eyes were moist and weeping she continued, "I am a bit crazy, I always say so many stupid things, please excuse me for being so talkative; it is not proper for a grown up woman like me!" We reached home and when I wanted to pay the rickshaw puller, she stopped me and said, "Not while I am around."

Aslam and I had only worked for two months when we got our notice of termination. All along Aslam kept his promise and shared his salary. I had also managed to earn some money by giving pastel sketches to a big British store, known as the Army and Navy Stores, where my paintings were displayed in the show window and I got 75% of the sale price.

Now with enough money to survive for more than six months, I thanked Thakur Singh gratefully for his hospitality, and took leave of my elder sister Banti, reconfirming my promised postcard. I rented a small room, a very small one at Tollygunj, agreeing to every condition of my landlord Banerjee Babu. I was anxious to be independent, indeed seriously so. One of my couplets expresses this feeling of independence thus *"Sir pay ahsaan na layta main kissi ka hasrat, mayray khandoon nay meri laash uthaye hooti"* (I would never accept any obligation, if only my shoulders could carry my corpse.) My pen name then was 'Hasrat'.

I learned that close to my place two Punjabi stalwarts, K.L.Saigal and Prithviraj Kapoor, were staying. They were working in New Theaters, where my idol Mr. D. K. Bose was making *Raj Rani Meera*. Both of them were actors, but not yet big stars. One Sunday morning I dressed up, once again as a dandy, and knocked at Prithviraj's door. A little chubby boy of six or seven opened the door. He looked like an angel with big blue eyes, a fair complexion and silken hair, but with a naughty smile. He was Prithviraj's eldest son Ranbir Raj Kapoor, who later became a legend in Indian cinema. The little boy led me through the verandah-cum-kitchen into the bedroom where Prithviraj was busy playing the sitar. Being a *Pehalwan* (a body builder), he seemed to be choking and wrestling with the delicate instrument. The trembling sounds from the strings conveyed the agony of the instrument of Swaraswati, Goddess of learning and music.

He was busy with his daily *Riaz* or practice. Seeing me he signalled with his hand to come and sit near him, while his eyes were half closed in rapture, as he continued to punish the instrument; his powerful fingers throttling the delicate strings. Then in a low theatrical, resounding voice he said, "This is the raga *Bhairvi* — *Sada Suhagan*, and may I know who you are and what brings you here?" His manner was very Shakespearean.

I had already rehearsed what I was going to say so I began, "Mr, Kapoor, I am a poet, a playwright, a composer, and a stage actor. I have come from Amritsar, the land of the Golden Temple. I have just completed my Masters degree in English and I have travelled all the way to meet Mr. D.K. Bose. So please, being a Punjabi brother, could you introduce me to him?"

Prithviraj kept plucking away at the strings and then in a sweet voice said, "I wish I could help, but destiny is my master and it dictates all my actions, I am a poor puppet. I have already recommended my younger brother Trilok. I just can't add another name while seeking Mr. Bose's favour. Blood is thicker than water and so I regret I can't be of help but I suggest you go and see Mr. K.L. Saigal, who lives next door. Perhaps he can."

I inquired before I left. "Does Mr. Saigal have a younger brother too?"

Prithviraj smiled and said, "He has, a boy called Mahinder, who wants to be a tailor, not an actor... God wanted to make him a girl, but unfortunately he changed his mind and made him a boy."

I thanked Prithviraj and knocked at his neighbour's door. Mahinder Saigal opened it, and took me to his brother's room. It was also quite amusing to see K.L. Saigal, the great singer — the man who was called Mr. Golden Voice — holding two cucumbers, like dumbbells, exercising to build his muscles. He had a charming face attached to a skinny frail body. It occurred to me quite ironic that Prithviraj, the man with muscles, was practicing to be a musician, while Saigal, the man with a wonderful voice was training to develop muscles. There was no playback system in those days, so singing had to be live, and the singer thought that a better build would help him get better roles in films.

Much to my surprise, I was welcomed very warmly by Saigal. He stopped exercising and with a sweet smile said, "Please come in, let me change my clothes while you have tea." Mahinder brought me a cup of tea. Then Saigal entered wearing his kurta pajama and inquired, "Have you come from Jullunder?"

"No, from Amritsar," I replied. He then asked what had brought me to his *garib khana* or humble abode. I was thrilled to see that Saigal was so humble and gracious. While I had spoken in English with Prithviraj, I conversed in simple Punjabi with Saigal. I told him about my desire to join films and meet Mr. Bose. He said in a friendly tone, "Shri Prithviraj is a graduate; he can discuss art and philosophy; he is tall and handsome, and his vast experience on stage has made him a favorite of Mr. Debaki Bose. In contrast, I am just an ordinary person with no acting experience. I used to be a salesman and singing is my hobby which has brought me to New Theatres to act in films. In Mr. Bose's opinion I am only a bard. That is why in the movie *Puran Bhagat* he only let me sing a few songs. So under the circumstances I will not be able to ask him for a favour, but if I ask Mrs. Durga Khote, who has learnt music from me, to introduce my brother Kidar Nath to Mr. D. K. Bose, some good results are possible. Mrs. Khote is the leading lady in *Raj Rani Meera* and Mr. Bose has immense regard for her. She is a nice lady, who will not disappoint me, I think, because I am her Guru." I thankfully inquired, "When will you take me to Mrs. Khote?" Saigal stood up and said "Right now! She lives nearby in a posh locality, Mohani Mansion, come let us not waste time." So the kindhearted Saigal took me there and introduced me to the tall dignified lady, with that wonderful dimpled smile that added to her charm.

Mrs. Khote told Saigal. "Next Sunday D.K. Bose is coming to my house for lunch, to discuss a few scenes of *Raj Rani Meera*. That should take about an hour, and if Mr. Kidar Nath arrives at about 2:30 p.m. I will certainly introduce him to D.K.B. That's how they addressed Mr. Bose. Both Saigal and I thanked her before we took our leave. When we came down, I shook hands with the great Mr. Saigal and I promised to inform him about the outcome of my meeting with D.K.B. before we parted company.

Next Sunday was only seven days away but they seemed like an eternity to me. At last the moment arrived.

I reached Mrs. Khote's house exactly at 2:30 p.m. A maid opened the door and asked me to wait in the drawing room, as both Mrs. Khote and Mr. Bose had gone to see someone in the neighbourhood. I sat nervously waiting for their return. At last the bell rang and the maid servant informed Mrs. Khote that someone was waiting in the drawing room. I stood up respectfully as I heard the footsteps of the two, and I greeted them both with folded hands. Mrs. Khote introduced me saying, "D.K.B. this young man is a great admirer of yours. He has seen *Puran Bhagat* and has come all the way from Amritsar to see you. You'd better ask him why."

Mr. Bose was well dressed and carried a note book in his hand. He sat down and asked the maid, "Could you please get us some coffee with lots of sugar." Before the maid could answer Mrs. Khote said, "Coffee will be served in a few minutes exactly as you like it". Then Mr. Bose opened his snuff box and took a pinch of snuff, wiping the extra amount with the back of his hand and asked, "What did you like in *Puran Bhagat*? The performances or the music?" I replied, "Sir, I liked the direction the best. After having seen your movie I decided to become a film man, a dream merchant."

Mr. Bose continued, "The glamour of film attracts many people from all over India young man. Daily we meet many people who are nice looking and keen to join films. If you are given a chance what would you like to do?" Just then Mrs. Khote arrived since she was also keen to hear my response. I replied, "From a director to a coolie, I would accept any job, just to be in films." Mr. Bose smiled and said, "I think as a director I am still more experienced and capable than you, and as for being a coolie I think you are too weak for manual labor of that kind. I suggest that you go back home and continue your studies."

The maid brought three cups of coffee and handed them to us. Mr. Bose saw disappointment written all over my face and he asked. "Do you know any art which could introduce you to the film world?" I replied, "I am a good poet, a good painter, and I am a better photographer!" "That is good" said Mr. Bose "Next month I have the opportunity of making a film called *Seeta* so meet me in a month's time, and if you can convince me that you can handle a still camera I will take you in my unit — this of course is dependent on my getting the project."

I shot up and kissed his hand and said, "Sir, I am so thankful to you for your kindness."

He then turned to Mrs. Khote and said, "You know in order to enter films I too had to do a bit of this and that." I quipped "Me too Sir, I have also had to do a bit of this and that, but it seems that I have done more of that." Mr. Bose liked my sense of humor and asked, "Where do you live?" I replied "At 70 Rassa Road, near the bungalow of Mr. Dinsha Irani. " Bose asked "So is Mr. Dinsha Irani your neighbour?" "No," I replied, "He is my neighbour-in-law, there is a building in between our houses."

Mr. Bose laughed again and said, "I am afraid I am going to like you, you are quick with your spicy comments, and it makes talking to you enjoyable. I am not so funny and I depend on others to make me laugh." At this point Mrs. Khote interjected, "Mr. Kidar Nath, from today onwards you are just Kidar to us, and every Sunday at 2:30 you will come and visit my flat for a glass of milk, you need nourishment badly."

I was moved by her kindness and his generosity in accepting me. I said. "Actually I am a nobody, I can pretend..." Mr. Bose cut me short saying, "You may a be nobody today, but you have the makings of being a somebody, someday my boy, don't lose heart." Then Mrs. Khote added that she had instructed the maid to give me some milk and that I should come again next Sunday.

That particular Sunday was a memorable day for me. I had at last met the great Mr. Bose and he liked me. Mr. Bose was not very tall. Though he was not handsome, he was dark and quite attractive. He loved food and he loved it presented in a variety of ways. He laughed like a baby, was attracted by charming feminine faces and figures. He enjoyed humour and I will always consider him as one of the best film directors that India has produced. Then I visited Mr. Saigal to keep him posted. My friendship with Prithviraj and Saigal also developed and we would meet almost weekly. They did not feel that I had forced myself upon them.

The room I had rented was no more than 32 square feet. It had no window but it had two doors, one opened to the outside of the building and the other led to a verandah. With such limited space, at night I had to place my luggage and my utensils, my shoes and all my belongings, outside. Luckily the adjoining room was a cowshed with a couple of cows and a calf, and it also contained a big table which looked like an operating table that perhaps some doctor had forgotten. It was quite high but only 12 inches wide and about six feet long. I bought it from the landlord for Rs.10. I slept on this table for years and had to master the art of balancing, like a circus acrobat, to avoid falling off at night. With practice, I soon managed to master not falling too often onto the hard floor while I slept. The cows would look at me with curiosity whenever I landed on the floor with a thud.

The other creatures that kept me company were mosquitoes, and even though I did not have much fat or blood in my skinny body to offer them, it seemed they preferred me to my landlord, Mr. Bannerji, his son or his daughter. The mosquitoes were also very musical at night as they buzzed around my ears. But I soon got used to them. The other thing that I did not appreciate were the tasteless paintings on the walls of my room. I was instructed not to remove them. I hated them but had to look at them every morning. One of these paintings depicted a God seated on a throne asking his wife to sit on his lap. And another one was of the God Hanuman. The paintings offended my sense of taste and I felt that they were not only terribly executed, but in bad taste. I finally replaced them with my own paintings of our national heroes Chatrapati Shivaji and Rana Pratap. Two men of extreme courage and valour; these were my inspiration to conquer and move mountains.

My regular visits to the Army & Navy Stores helped me supplement my income. And my visits to Prithviraj and Saigal helped cement a great friendship among the three of us. While Saigal was a man of few words, Prithviraj in comparison loved to talk, and we would converse for hours. Prithviraj became my real buddy. He could deliver a lecture on any subject, while I could concoct stories and tell him interesting yarns that were engrossing and entertaining. Prithviraj enjoyed my verse, my humour and our conversations. Time passed and made my poverty more bearable. I was alone, away from my friends, my family and my beloved wife. What I missed most was her support, and gentleness. "Nothing is so strong as gentleness, nothing is so gentle as real strength." – Ralph W. Sockman. Years later I wrote, *Mayray khaloon main aa kur galay lagaaja mujhey, kay aaj phir mera dil*

Chahata hai roonay ko... (embrace me in my dreams, today, again I feel like weeping).

CHAPTER 8

"The road to wisdom? – Well, it's plain and simple to express: Err and err and err again, But less and less and less."

Piet Hein

Mr. Bose's plans to direct *Seeta* materialized with the East India Film Company, and the producer Mr. B.L. Khemka agreed to all the terms imposed by Mr. Bose. Durga Khote was to play the main female lead and Prithviraj, with special permission from New Theatres, was the main male star. I was hired as promised, to become the still photographer. At last two of my wishes had come true. I would work with my idol Mr. Bose, and I had at last got a job in tinsel town. I knew that I was an amateur because I had only learned to handle a box camera during my college days in Amritsar. I knew nothing about the field camera which was used professionally, nor much about the new panchromatic emulsion film. I had only used orthochromatic film till now.

I dressed up in my Sunday best, like some foreign returned young man, polished up my English, and feeling assured of my ability to express myself, was confident of convincing everybody that I knew my job very well. My biggest asset has been my confidence. As a painter, I could always compose better than most people, so I thought I would master the art of photography quite soon, of course not without trial and error.

Now Dass Babu, the head of still photography, disliked me from the very beginning, his grudge being my attire, my fluent English, and my closeness to Mr. D. K. Bose. At that time in East India Studios, Mr. Bose, Durga Khote, Prithviraj, and Kidar were called the 'Gang' and the 'Four Musketeers'. Soon, on an auspicious day, the shooting started and I was thrilled by the proceedings.

After a while I was asked to take a few stills, with full freedom to recompose for better visual effects. Mr. Bose liked my skill and style and my ability to take total command. Actually I was just dramatizing to impress my audience. We shot till lunch, and since part of the set was still being completed by the twenty or so carpenters, we were instructed that we would resume after 9:00 pm. when the balance of the set would be complete. Mr. Bose was the first Indian Director who wanted to create the effect of a storm at night by using the propeller of a tiger moth airplane. The entire unit decided to stay in the studio to resume work late at night.

Wearing slacks had just become fashionable, and Mrs. Khote, after dinner, intended to wear a pair when her tailor

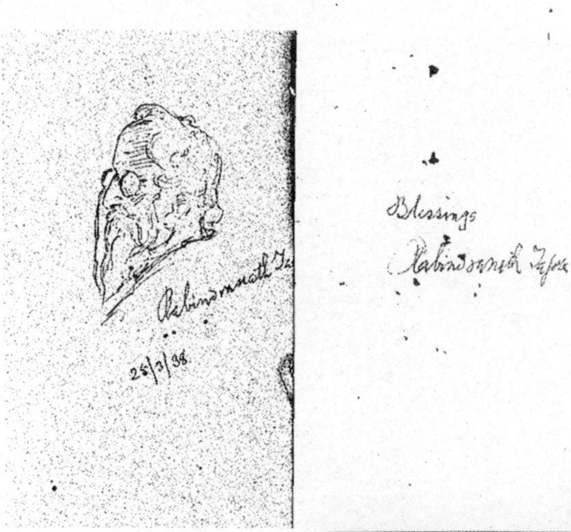

I hastily sketchedon the manuscript of my book of poems 'Punchi'. Gurudev Rabindranath Tagore autographed it with his blessings.

My sketch of Sharat Chander Chatterjee appeared in a Bengali magazine.

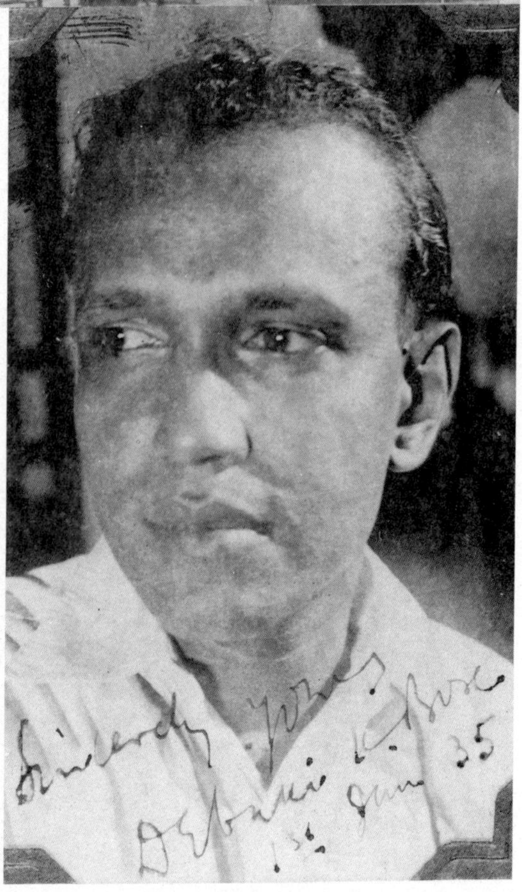

Working in New Theatre with my Guru D.K. Bose (left) was a magical time for me.I was fully immersed in allphases of the business. Besides writing and photography I also got bit parts.

opp. pg.
As a butler, and (below) with the great singer K.C. Dey

During the time of my struggle in Calcutta, I lost so much weight, that I began to Iook like a skeleton. The doctor diagnosed that I had holes in the intestine. He advised me to go back home since I might not have much longer to live.

Cast as the female lead, in one of the many college plays that I had written, produced and directed. Me as an actor. *The Educated Wife* was an instant hit. So much so that the play was even printed.

I got married to the most beautiful Raj Dulari. She was unique in her constant support for me.
"Any woman, if she loves, gives a man a sense of the infinite." – Jules Michelet

brought it. But she hesitated. Mr. Bose insisted that she try it out so we could all see the new style, that modern girls were wearing. So Mrs. Khote went to the make-up room with her maid while we waited outside. Twenty minutes later the maid came out and said that Mrs. Khote needed a belt and had asked me to lend her my belt.

Being very thin I used my belt to ensure that my trousers kept me company, because without them we were both lost. But now that Mrs. Khote had asked and Mr. Bose ordered that I give it to her, I obeyed. I unfastened the belt and gave it to the maid servant, holding on to my trousers with both my hands, and hoping that after everyone had observed the latest fashion of women in slacks, my belt would be returned. But things took a different turn. As soon as Mrs. Khote appeared everybody complimented her, saying that she looked as elegant as any foreigner. Mr. Bose then took her aside towards his car and the two of them disappeared. I was left holding my pants. Everyone dispersed, and when Prithviraj passed by me he smiled and said, "They have gone to Chowrangee, and they will be back in a couple of hours. Mr. Bose has taken her to the market to buy her a new belt." So, I waited under a big tree holding my pants and waited for the two of them to return.

Dass Babu, head of the still department, finding me in this funny position, smiled and left. Soon I heard people from across the road open their windows and I could hear the sound of giggles. I knew I was in a very embarrassing position and could not let go of my pants. This was one time I did not want to be caught with my pants down.

Hours passed, before Mr. Bose at last returned. Mrs. Khote had gone home to get ready for the night shoot. He saw my anguish and understood the predicament I was in but he just smiled in sympathy and said, "So, you...?" and I responded "Yes. Sir for several hours now." He then asked his driver to get me a rope to replace my belt and to take me to the nearest restaurant to at least have dinner before we resumed shooting.

When we returned I was thrilled to see the preparations for the storm scene being enacted for the first time in Indian Movies. Everything looked so real. Sebta (Mrs. Khote's nickname) was given full instructions to follow a particular path. The entire crew was very excited. The camera lay hidden in a pit in the ground. Suddenly, the propellers of the plane swung into action. Trees swung, branches shook, leaves flew, the wind howled like a real storm playing havoc with whatever came it its way.

Soon a signal was given for lights. They came on, and the propeller was now picking up speed making the blades invisible. Soon we heard the word "Camera", and two cameras started rolling. It was a rare sight. As I watched, I noticed that the leaves and small twigs flying past the propeller had been exhausted. No one but me seemed to have noticed, that there were no more leaves or twigs in this raging storm. I quickly collected some leaves and shrubs in my arms and was about to release them in front of the moving blades of the propeller. But I could not see the blades which were moving so rapidly, they were invisible. Suddenly there was a shriek.

Mr. Bose's hawk eyes had seen that if I were to take another step I would have been in the path of the blades, and would have been sliced to bits. He ran towards me, pulled me back with all his force and threw me to the ground. Everybody became aware of the averted tragedy. Mr. Bose was furious and began to curse me in Bengali saying, "It was none of your business to improve the effect of the storm. That is the Art Director's job and my concern, not my still photographer's responsibility. You would have been chopped to bits had I not noticed and pulled you back in time." I realized how close I had come to death, had I taken just one more step; another situation where God had saved me from an awful death. Suddenly the lights were turned off and the propeller whirred to a slow stop, and I became the centre of embarrassing attention. Mrs. Khote remarked that she shuddered to think what would have happened. Prithviraj held my trembling hand and took me away so I would not be reprimanded any more. Soon Mr. Bose said: "Cancel the shooting tonight, I am in no mood to shoot."

My dear friend Prithviraj made me sit on a bench and looking me straight in the eye said, "Kidar you would have been shredded to bits with your blood all over this man-made jungle. Tonight the dream of the dream merchant would have ended. Your loss would mean nothing to the film industry but for your old parents and your young wife, waiting to hear some good news, it would have been a shattering tragedy". That night Prithviraj gave me a lift home on his bicycle, and I felt that even the cows near my bed looked at me with sad eyes. I quietly went to sleep on my high table and I am sure that one of them licked my feet with affection.

Twenty four hours later, we resumed shooting the storm scene, but I noticed that a fencing had been built around the blades of the propeller. We worked all night and completed the entire storm sequence. I had the opportunity to take a dozen shots of the filming. And then we were told to take rest and report the next morning.

In the morning when I reached the studio the first person I met was Dass Babu who with a grin said "Mr. Bose is waiting for you in Mr. Khemka's office, he wants to see you at once." I thought perhaps he had seen the prints I had exposed, and he was going to complement me on my excellent work. I knew that Mr. Khemka was a shrewd businessman. He had learned English and was very careful with both his money and his language. If you greeted him he would not acknowledge it because he thought it was beneath his dignity to respond. He just stared back without blinking an eye. He loved to be seen as a stern formidable boss to his lowly employees.

When I entered, I greeted them both, but they were both stony faced. Then Mr. Khemka with suppressed anger said. "These are the twelve negatives exposed by you, but not one of them has an image on them. These are twelve transparent pieces of glass, what do you have to say?" Besides this he said something in his own language (Marwari) which I cannot translate because it was all Greek to me but it sounded like an abuse.

I held the transparencies to the light and replied, "They are as clear as my conscience", because I knew that Dass Babu had finally got his revenge. The negatives had never been processed properly but simply dipped in hypo solution which gave them that transparent look. My heart sank because I was being ridiculed and Mr. Dass had finally done me in.

Mr. Bose took the hint and asked, "You mean to say that you have been sabotaged?" "Yes, Sir." I replied, "otherwise there would have been some trace of an image, some highlight, these plates have not been processed, but have simply been dipped in hypo and fixed, to get me into trouble." Mr. Bose stood up and said, "Go and expose two stills of Ram (Prithviraj), who is ready with his make-up, then I want you to process the pictures yourself and bring them to me. I want you to prove your innocence or else I will have to punish you." His comment was loud enough for Dass to hear everything.

I went to do as I was told, to salvage my honour. I exposed two negatives of Prithviraj and took the slides to the darkroom, where Dass Babu was waiting. He said in a sarcastic voice, "Here is the bottle of developer, if you know what that is. It is made by Kodak and not by me. The tanks contain hypo and the fixative. This is the lamp, and there is a clock." I did not like him to lecture me so I simply closed the door, switched on the lamp and began wondering what to do next. I knew I was not really a professional photographer but was just trying hard. I had developed some orthochrome negative film under a red light, but under what kind of light was one supposed to develop panchromatic emulsion? I had no clue.

I decided to process everything in total darkness, to be on the safe side. But I had no idea how long I was supposed to keep the film in the developer, nor could I see the clock which just ticked away in the darkness. I was nervous. It was like a nightmare, an ordeal. Suddenly I remembered my grandmother's words — 'Whenever you are in difficulty and need God's help, sing with full devotion, this Bhajan:' "*Nath Tu Nay Ghhaj Ke Band Chudaye*" — and God will help you. I remembered my grandmother's advice to send an S.O.S. to the Master for divine help.

I turned off all the lights, put the negatives in the developer, shaking it while I sang my *Bhajan* (prayer). When the prayer ended I assumed that the developing time was over. I took the negatives out in the darkness and one by one rinsed them in cold water and then dipped them in hypo and waited. All I could hear was the ticking of the clock and the beating of my heart. After about ten minutes, still sweating, I took them out with my trembling hands, and switched on the light to see what destiny had in store for me. Slowly my eyes adjusted to the light, and leisurely they brought into focus two brilliant negatives, with every sharp detail. It was a miracle. I washed them hurriedly and ran to Mr. Bose, who took me personally to Mr. Khemka's office. I had been vindicated. Mr. Khemka again started with some verbal assault in Marwari, which again I could not understand, or translate, looked at the negatives and said "Good," stretching his words to add some sort of emphasis, but before he could say another word I blurted out, "Then goodbye, I have proved my innocence and my capability. I do not want to work here any longer. I am handing in my resignation, please advise the accountant to clear my dues." Mr. Bose and Khemka both told me not to get so emotional, and asked me to continue my job as a still photographer, but I was adamant. I was paid about Rs. 110 for one month and one week's employment, and I swore never to enter that studio again. Destiny had taken some radical turns in those few days. On Friday my life was saved and on Monday although I had salvaged my honour, I was once again unemployed.

Next Sunday as usual I went to Mrs. Khote's flat and was glad to see Mr. Bose and Prithviraj. Mr. Bose congratulated me for my courage saying, "I am happy to see that Kidar is bold enough not to bow before Insolent Might, I wish I too had the gall." Mr. Bose also promised that he would hire me when he had completed negotiating with New Theatres for his up-coming movie *After the Earthquake*. And Prithviraj asked me to visit him more often because his son Raju (Ranbir Raj a.k.a. Raj Kapoor) was very proud of his Uncle Sharma. In his opinion I was a genius, who could write, compose music and make people laugh with my silly anecdotes and observations, but above all he was proud that I had the strength of moral character and conviction, to stand up and not follow the rest like sheep. "Uncle Sharma is a lion" he said, "loyal and lofty." Since I am a Leo I was quite proud of what he said.

After months of unemployment there was finally a ray of hope. Mr. Bose had completed *Seeta* and was to go back to New Theatres to start his next movie '*After The Earthquake*'. He mentioned that there was no job available as a still photographer, but advised me to join as a painter and junior artist. I agreed, and for the first time I was allowed to enter the gates of New Theatres, after always having been shunted away by the Pathan gatekeeper.

At New Theatres my old associates, Mrs. Khote, Prithviraj, and Saigal were glad to see me as a member of the New Theatres' family. New Theatres was the busiest studio in those days. It was a wonderful period, the golden days of the film industry. Here I also met such greats as the blind singer K.C. Dey, later his nephew Manna Dey also became a famous singer, and the very talented music director R.C. Boral to whom the film industry will always be indebted for the wonderful music he has provided all those years. I also met a very interesting actor Mr. Nawab Kashmiri who liked me for my poetry. Mr. Kashmiri hailed from Lucknow, like another famous singer-actor Pahari Sanyal.

Mr. Bose, also let me play a small comic role in his movie, but I was required to bring my own woolen trousers for the role. The first day's shooting was a party scene, and after the day's work the man in-charge of the wardrobe insisted that I leave my gray woolen trousers behind since it was part of the movie, and he needed it for continuity. He promised it would be returned after the scene was completed, and I willingly obliged.

Now I was earning Rs 100 per month and so could afford to send Rs 30 to my father who was jobless, and had to move back to Narowal. Rs. 100 was a good salary in those days, it seemed like a lot of money. I was happy, everyone was friendly with me, I felt I was on cloud nine.

On Dewali day I was invited to a party, so I decided to dress up like a dandy, but I needed my gray trousers from the man in-charge of the wardrobe. I promised him that I would return it the next night, and after much coaxing he finally agreed and handed me a box with my trousers freshly laundered and pressed.

I wore a crisp white shirt which had been starched and pressed and put on my gray woolen trousers, and the best bow tie I had. From my single bulb lit room I wished the cows a Happy Dewali before locking the door to go to the party. Whistling I decided to first go and wish Mrs. Khote. I was in a good mood and swaggered along, but I could feel the presence of someone following me. I could hear the giggles from the street urchins who seemed to be tagging behind me. At first I failed to see what was funny. I stopped whistling and started walking a bit slower, but the chuckles continued. I knew that they were laughing at me. Cautiously I felt behind my back to discover that my stiffly starched shirt struck out from a large hole in my pants, just like a bunny rabbits tail. It then dawned on me that during the party scene while filming the movie, I must have sat down on some sweets, and after the shooting the wardrobe man must have left the trousers hanging in the studio, and the rats must have had a good feast and had nibbled away part of my trousers. The following day the trousers must have gone to the laundry and the hole was completely unnoticed. My evening was ruined, I could not go to the party on this holy day with a holey pant, so tucking the shirt back in I marched, no almost ran, back to my room with the children mocking and chasing me all the way home.

The next day I approached Mr. Bose and explained the situation to him hoping to be compensated for the hole in my trousers. He said, "How do you figure it was the work of the rats?" To which I shot back. "I assure you I did not eat any gun powder to have caused such a big hole through my pants." He laughed and had the cashier reimburse me Rs. 20 not only for my trousers, but also for my remark.

That night also I decided to visit my friends, Prithviraj Kapoor and K.L. Saigal to wish them a happy Dewali. First I visited Prithviraj and after exchanging pleasantries I went and knocked on Saigal's door.

They say that alcohol and eloquence have a harmonious relationship; that night both flowed freely. Shri Saigal it seemed had drunk more than his usual, and though not drunk, he was in a reminiscing mood and needed company, even if it was the company of a teetotaler.

In his mellow voice he started relating an episode from his past. He said that when he was a typewriter salesman, he also sold cotton saris to supplement his income. He then told me the story of a young girl called Najma. He told me that he had hired a coolie who helped him carry the load of cotton saris as they moved from one poor locality to another through the slums of Calcutta. In one of these places he encountered a naughty but charming girl Najma who would always stop him and ask to see the same green sari that she loved. "I always showed her other sarees", he said, but there was one particular sari she had set her heart on. The green one, but it cost ten rupees. One day she said to me, "I am an orphan, with no mother and father and I doubt if I even have Allah to protect me, but I do have my Dada (an elder brother), who will get paid next Friday. So please don't sell that particular sari till that day and we hope to have the money then to buy it from you." I promised her that I would put that sari aside and bring it back on the following Friday.

That Friday I was eager to make little Najma happy and I went back to her colony, but I did not hear the shrill voice of Najma calling out to me as she always did. Surprised, I went to her hut to remind her of her promise. When I entered I found her elder brother Irshad sobbing like a child. When I inquired what was wrong, he replied, "Last night Najma had complained about some chest pains. So I called the doctor who had charged me Rs 15 for the visit, but by the time he got here, she had died of an heart attack — my Najma is lying inside and I do not even have any money for her *Kafan* (shroud)." I then told him that I had a green sari which she liked very much, and as her brother I wanted to give her this sari. Najma was clad in that green sari and went heavenwards without saying goodbye. I stopped selling saris from that day onwards," said Saigal.

Now, during those days I used to travel by tram car to the studio which was located at some distance. One day I felt that all eyes were focused not only on me, but in particular on my lap. Behind me stood a young attractive college student. I was too embarrassed to look down. It seemed the object of their stare was a white handkerchief that the young girl had accidentally dropped, and which had landed squarely on my lap. I had not noticed the object fall, and the young miss was too shy to ask me for her handkerchief. I tried to keep my head up and slyly peeped down at my lap. Seeing a white object on my lap, I thought a part of my shirt was sticking out of my trousers, and so very secretly I placed my hands on my lap and then in a flash I opened my fly and shoved the handkerchief inside my pant. The girl was aghast and the other passengers started snickering. When I got up, the little miss looked at me with repulsion and said, "Pervert." The crowd burst into gales of laughter. I stepped off the tram, as the laughter and the tram faded away in the distance.

I went behind a tree to examine the contents of my pants more thoroughly, and in private, when to my surprise I discovered that the white object was not my shirt but the girl's handkerchief. She had been too shy to pick it up herself or ask me for it, but when I tucked it into my pants she was horrified. I did not know how to return the well perfumed object, and so I just put it in my pocket.

Since I was living alone and had overlooked my dietary habits, I constantly suffered from abdominal ailments. Eventually it was diagnosed that I suffered from chronic dysentery, and was asked to go to the Tropical School of Medicine for a check-up, and advice. I was reluctant, but my friend Prithviraj insisted and said that it was not something that I could ignore, since it could be very serious. They kept me at the place for a whole day, washed my stomach and performed various tests and X-rays and said I should report back in a couple of days. When I returned the doctor gave me a sealed envelope and a look of sympathy, saying, "Give this to your doctor", then he asked me, "Do you have any relatives?" "Yes," I replied, "I have my parents, two brothers a sister as well as a young wife and a baby boy called Bitto, but they are all in the Punjab." The doctor then said, "I advise you to go back to your relatives and then come back for a long and expensive treatment." Just then the phone rang and the doctor left. I sensed that what the doctor was suggesting was that I should bid everyone goodbye before my tragic end which was in sight.

My own doctor confirmed my worst fears when he read the concealed contents of the envelope and checked my X-ray. He said, "I am going to be frank with you. Your intestines have holes and since surgery is not possible, the disease is eating away the lining of your intestine and…if…maybe," he had started to fumble for words, when I asked. "How long do I have to live." He said.

"A patient in your condition has a few weeks — eight may be ten, twelve at the very most."

That night I felt sad for myself and could not sleep, I thought I would die without achieving my goal. I remembered the immortal lines by Iqbal. *"Bagh-e-bahisht say mujhe, rakhtey sufarr diya the kiyun? Kar-e-jahaan daraaz hai, aab mera inttzar kur."* (Was it not You, who ordered me out from the garden of Eden? My tasks on earth are still in progress, now You wait till I am ready). I had restricted my diet to yogurt as advised by my doctor. I lay awake on the high but narrow table, even the cows avoided staring at me that night. Soon one cow came and started licking my foot and I thought, "Why, is this mute animal doing this? Does she know that it is time for us to say goodbye, or is she expressing her love and concern?" I patted the animal and shifted my table out of her reach.

As I lay down, my thoughts shifted to my family. My father was an old and tired man, my mother an old uneducated religious woman, my two younger brothers — the monkeys who liked me so much. My sister Guro who was now married, but who tied a *Rakhi* (a sacred thread) on my wrist every year, must now be waiting for this coming *Rakhi* day which was fast approaching. And finally my thoughts turned to my little son and my silent, sweet and sincere wife who never asked any questions, nor ever made any demands. She had loaned me the Rs. 25 hu I needed when I left home to pursue my dreams.

The next day I wrote an application for three week's leave of absence without pay, booked my ticket to Narowal and headed home. I had no money to buy anyone a present. I felt ashamed. Prithviraj had suggested that he could loan me Rs. 100 but I declined saying I did not need financial help. I lied. I also lied about my chronic ailment and the dangerous condition my health was in. I mentioned it to nobody. I said that I was returning to attend a marriage back home.

After a long and tiring journey I reached Amritsar, and without meeting any of my old friends. I left the same day for my village Narowal. I had not written to anyone about visiting home, so when I did reach, everyone was overjoyed. They rushed to greet me at the main gate, and when my father looked at me he said. "What is wrong with you? Are you sick?" I told him that I had dysentery, but instead of panicking he simply said. "No problem. Tomorrow I will take you to see Haji Abbas. My mother brought some *isabgol* and insisted that I take a dose of it in her presence with *Misri Sharbat* — a local drink.

My father said. "Congratulations, for earning such a big salary." No one in our family has ever made one hundred rupees, but then no one in our family ever went to college. They did not know that my education had not helped me, but my skill as a painter had. They also thought that Calcutta was a city like Amritsar, where the people were still simple village folk. They took pride in the stories I related. I rediscovered that they loved me immensely.

Next day my father took me to Haji Abbas who was not a Hakim but a businessman in the brick manufacturing business, and had some kilns, in which he baked bricks. When my father told him about my chronic dysentery the Haji said. "Punditji I do know one *Nuskha* (prescription) but the medicine is costly, it will cost at least Rs. 1 and it takes four days for preparation in earthen pots, with various ingredients which have to be fired in kilns. Tomorrow we will be starting kiln No. 3." My father requested that he write out the ingredients and herbs required. Haji Abbas added, "The boy will require 7 doses and I will therefore keep half the medicine for some other poor people who can't afford the expensive herbs." "Do as you please, as long as my Kidar is cured." Said my father. Haji Sahib nodded with the words. "*Insha Allah*." (God's will)

On the fifth day my father went early in the morning to Haji Abbas and collected the charcoal like powder and put it in a glass ampule. In those days no one had heard of a capsule, so Haji Abbas had devised his own method. He instructed my father. "*Take dehi ki malaiee* (crust of curds) and then with the uncoated end of a matchstick sprinkle just a gram of the medicine on it and let your son gulp the curds, and then drink a glass of *lassi*." (buttermilk).

It was a miracle. After the fifth dose I was completely cured! God knows how, the holes in my intestines must have healed by those few grams of burnt charcoal herbs. My appetite also improved and I started gaining weight. My people knew that I should be going back to Calcutta, so my mother suggested that I should take my wife along because now that I was employed it was only proper. She said. "Your wife should not be a burden to her own parents, it is not proper, so please go to your in-laws place in Rawalpindi and take her and your son with you to Calcutta."

I obeyed my mother and after a few days, my wife and I took a train for the long journey. I told her. "You will be living not in a room, but in a special nest. I will ensure that I find some comfortable accommodation for you and our son." Wives in those days only listened, they never argued, so now Mr. & Mrs. Kidarnath started living in Calcutta, and somehow managed to rent the extra, small attached room at my old place.

Call it Divine Help, or destiny, the publicity officer of New Theatres was very impressed by the layout of my posters and he offered to pay me Rs. 40 per poster design of 30" x

40" size and Rs. 90 for a single sheeter of 40" x 60". The extra income made life a bit more comfortable for us, but I still slept in the company of cows on the high table.

Mr. D.K. Bose got an offer from Bombay, when his film was nearing completion, and he asked if I would like to continue as a member of his unit. I enthusiastically replied, "Yes, Sir, I would like to stick with you but there is a minor problem, and you may solve it for me. Today I am asking you for something." He replied, "Ask and I shall try to oblige." I told him as meekly as I could. that I was a married man and that there may soon be an addition in the family. So, I wanted him to give me an increment of Rs.5 only, to make my salary Rs. 105.

Suddenly Mr. Bose became very sarcastic and said, "You desire Rs.5 more? If so, then you must first deserve it." That was the moment when I knew that Kidarnath was born in this very timid and meek frame. I told Mr. Bose, "I hope I shall prove that what I deserve may be a 100% or perhaps even a 1000% more! Time alone will prove my prophecy right." Mr. Bose was offended but I was hurt. A poem echoed through my head. *"Khuda say maang tujhe maangna hai jo akbar, yeh woh maqaam hai zillat nahin sawaal kay baad." (Ask of God whatever you need, there is no degradation thereafter)."*

Time passed. I continued to be a faithful worker of New Theatres. I continued to day-dream. Luckily, Prithviraj was there to encourage me at every step.

Chapter 9

"An opportunity does not make a hero, it only reveals one."

One day it was raining very heavily — cats and dogs, as they say. But duty is duty. I set forth to reach New Theatres in time. I was walking in the heavy rain, drenched to the bone. I had no umbrella or raincoat. I did not have these luxuries. Just the will to walk to my destination. As I was walking along, I heard a car honk, and thinking that the motorist needed more space on the flooded road, I shifted to one side. But the car kept on honking. So I moved to the very edge of the road, but the honking persisted. I looked to see who was blowing the horn, and I was amazed to find Mr. B.N. Sircar, the owner of New Theatres, driving his latest car and signalling for me to get in. I was puzzled. Was Mr. Sircar really offering me a lift in his posh new car? I was just a bit employee, and a screen painter.

When I was sure that Mr. Sircar really wanted to give me a lift on this stormy day, I approached the car and tried to open the door, but it had no handle. It had some kind of a button. Poor me, I could not locate this magic button, so

I said loudly, "Open Sesame! Open Sesame!" This amused Mr. Sircar and he opened the door for me saying, "Hop in. You will fall sick if you expose yourself to the storm."

I jumped into the car, and we headed towards the studio. God knows why I said to Mr. Sircar, "Sir, do you remember what Lord Clive, one day, said to his officers?" Mr. Sircar inquired, "What did Lord Clive say?" I replied, "He said, take away my pen and give me a sword and I will prove my worth." So, I continued saying, "Please take away my brush and give me a pen, and I will also prove myself too." But before Mr. Sircar could comment, we reached the studio.

The old Pathan, the gate-man, who had generally shooed me away many a time from the gate, with abusive language, saw me today in the company of the big boss. He saluted Mr. Sircar and perforce had to salute me too. This was a most amazing feeling for me. Although Mr. Sircar had made no commitment about giving me a chance to write dialogue or songs for New Theatres, I sensed that destiny had opened a new door for me.

Soon I learned from Mr. Boral and Mr. Hemchander that Mr. Sircar, who was a great wit, himself, was amused by my remark, "Open Sesame", and was pleased to know that I was well-educated, well-behaved and well-informed. Next day, dressed in my best clothes, I went to his office and said, "Sir, belonging is quite different from just being employed. I am unable to manage on the present salary and so I need a raise." Mr. Sircar responded, "For that you will have to see Mama Babu! Wait – I shall give you a note and you may go and see him right now, because he is in a good mood today."

So, armed with Mr. Sircar's note, I went to see the gentleman. He saw the note and smiled. So did I. He looked at me for a long time and then burst into laughter and said, "Last night I saw the rushes of *After the Earthquake*. Are you the same funny man who plays the comic role of the domestic servant?" My reply was, "Yes, Sir." He said, still laughing, "Debaki Babu's comedy is usually more pathetic and much more boring, but this time you and your funny song made me laugh and laugh – yes, I have read the note you have just brought. For how long have you been paid the salary of Rs. 100?" I replied, "Ever since I joined New Theatres." Mama Babu thought for a while and said, "Look, this is the month of August, so from July onwards your salary will be raised to Rs. 200 per month. And after six months, your salary from January onwards will be Rs. 300 per month. I hope you are satisfied. "I was so moved by his generosity that I was silent and only nodded my head. I left his office after saluting him respectfully, for this most magnificent gesture.

Those were the days when New Theatres brought glory to the Indian Cinema with a galaxy of talented stars, thinkers, writers, poets, who assembled at this great studio. New Theatres made movies like *Chandidas, Puran Bhagat, Devdas*, etc. etc., because Mr. B.N. Sircar had pledged to improve the standard of Indian Cinema. Mr. Sircar was a thorough gentleman. He descended from a very rich and noble family, had been educated abroad, and was very witty, with a subtle sense of humour, what we call 'British Humor'. Brevity is the soul of wit, they say, and Mr. Sircar personified this with his pithy comments and remarks. I have seldom met a man who said so much in such few words.

When his agent from Punjab, Mr. Kazi, decided to build an independent studio of his own at Lahore, Mr. Sircar was invited for the opening ceremony. After the cutting of the ribbon, Mr. Sircar was invited to speak. He made a rare speech of only three words. He said, "Kazi, follow me." And he walked off the stage followed by others, another example of his brevity.

Director Amar Malik, who was very fat, funny looking and very dark skinned, one winter got a woollen jacket stitched from a very fashionable tailoring shop. He wore it with pride, and wanting to show off, told Mr. Sircar, "This expensive jacket has a silver lining, just see", and he showed him the inner lining. Mr. Sircar quietly remarked, "Every dark cloud has one too." Everyone sitting in his office had a hearty laugh and Mr. Malik became silent.

Sharat Chandra Chatterji, the renowned novelist had written *Devdas*. I had made a sketch of him which was printed in a Bengali magazine. Mr. Barua had filmed Devdas in Bengali, and it proved to be a huge, smashing success. So, New Theatres had decided to make the Hindi version too, with Mr. K.L. Saigal as Devdas, and Mr. Barua as the director. Destiny again played a beautiful card to help me score another victory. In spite of everyone's warning, I was chosen by Mr. Sircar to write the dialogue and lyrics for Devdas. The one man who told Mr. Sircar that Kidar was the only man who could do justice to this assignment was Saigal. He told Mr. Sircar, "I have read his poems and he is a genius." This film became an all-time classic!

"What marks the artist is his power to shape the material of pain we all have." – Lionel Trilling. Years later I wrote *"Mu chuppaye darrd nikla, loag sumjhey geet hai"* which contained similar sentiments.

Although, I had been writing for a long time, occasionally furiously, only part of my work, was known to people. *Devdas* was my first commissioned writing assignment, my real contribution to Indian movies. I had changed the very style of writing for films. Dialogue, the style of the theatre, had persisted in films, I had changed that to sound more natural, more like the language of the common people.

When *Devdas* was ready, one of the distributors felt that another song should be inserted, because the narrative was probably jumpy. There was no time at all. That night Saigal and I sat down, and I tried to write a song, appropriate for the situation. Although Saigal was not the music director, he worked at composing the music. The next morning this song was picturized, and Saigal sang the haunting, *"Dukh kay aab din beetat naahin, sukh kay din thay aik swapan the, aab din beetat naahin moore aab din beetat naahin."* With the release of *Devdas*, I was acknowledged as a great pen. The songs, *"Dukh kay aab din beetat naahin"* and *"balam aaye baso moray munmain"* were super hits. I was finally acclaimed, by the press, public and my parents.

Both, Bimal Roy and I, both got our first big break in *Devdas*. He as the cameraman, and I the writer. I moved away from Calcutta earlier, and years later he also moved to

Bombay to direct and produce some outstanding films. Our paths crossed many a time, and there was a sense of rivalry but a healthy respect for each other.

Mama Babu kept his word. The salary envelope I received had the extra amount in July. This made my wife and me very happy, and that much more comfortable. As promised my salary was further raised to Rs. 300 by Mama Babu. I felt the birth of a daughter would really bring me luck. With the extra money I no longer had to sleep on a 12" wide high table, in the company of my landlord's cows, and was able to indulge in the luxury of renting the first floor which had four bedrooms, a separate kitchen, two bathrooms, two balconies and a large passage for just Rs. 75 per month, despite my wife advising me to be thrifty.

My father's predictions, about the luck a girl in the family would bring, became a reality. When my father heard of the birth of a daughter, he wrote back, "Hearty Congratulations, this little girl is the luckiest person in our family, she will bring you unexpected fame and fortune, and is very lucky for all of us. But specially, for her father. When you name her, do it beginning with a letter 'P'. Wherever she goes, prosperity will accompany her." This is why the little brat was named, Prabha. As a baby she cried the loudest in our family. Our maid servant adored her, and Prabha learned to speak chaste Bengali as she grew up.

When my salary increased three fold, my domestic problems also multiplied. There was a letter from my father, saying he had borrowed some money from his relatives, who insisted on receiving payment and interest every month, to the tune of Rs. 100 per month. My financial condition needed to be changed. I had to augment my monthly earnings, so I requested Mr. Saigal to use my songs for his private gramophone recordings with the local company called, 'The Hindustan Recording Company'. He was kind enough to recommend my name and I was offered Rs.5 per song. I agreed. I wrote several songs for the company, which recorded Mr. Saigal's private numbers.

I received only Rs. 5 for such famous songs, as *"Suno suno hay krishan kala"* and *"Panchee kahe hoat uddas."* One of my ghazals he sang is partly reproduced here, *"Shamma ka jalna hai ya sozzashe purwana hai, chhand lafzon may yahhi ishaq ka afsaana hai. -- yeh janoon hai kay yahaantuk mera bhad jaye janoon, hans kay deewanagi keh daay kay yeh deewana hai – dil shikasta leiya baitha hai umangoon ka hajoom, ek tootay huye paymaney main*

Mehkhanna hai. – aabla dil key tassali kay leiya hai hasrat, yahi saagar, yahi shisha, yahi paymanna hai." My nom de plume then was Hasrat. But beggars cannot be choosers, and I also accepted an offer to paint posters for the publicity officer of New Theatres, to earn some extra money.

Time passed. I was more comfortable. My baby boy, Vikram, was a toddler and a source of joy and inspiration. I had rented a big flat with six rooms. Even my parents felt, I had some status now. I even affixed a name plate on the door of my flat. There was one small room, which I used as my studio for painting and writing. I could not afford to buy an easel or a palette, so I had to make do without these essentials. I used the floor for mixing paint, and I would also spread the poster on the floor to work on it, since I could not afford a drawing board.

One day when I had finished a 40" x 60" poster, I let it dry on the floor. It was a very large face of Umashashi, the big star. The next day, when I went to this small room, I was shocked to find her face looking like Charlie Chaplin's. There was an addition of a Hitler-type mustache on her upper lip. Soon the mystery was solved by a child's giggle. Vikram had spilled some black colour on the floor, smeared his tiny feet with wet paint and just walked across the face of the big star.

I was not amused. I was furious. I could not bear to see my work go down the drain. The animal in me chased the little culprit, who was hiding behind the door, and when I caught him I slapped him hard, twice. I think my children have inherited their ego from me. The little chap stared back with dignity, his little lips twisting but he refrained from crying. He rushed to me and clung to my neck. I suddenly relaxed and smearing his little fingers with yellow paint, I rubbed his smeared hands over my forehead and my cheeks, and then yelled to call his loving mother for help. When my wife came running and I told her the whole story, she picked up her pet in her arms and said, "Come Bittu, we will have kutti (we are not on speaking terms) with your Papa. He is a heartless and thoughtless man and we will never enter his studio again." I realized my mistake and promised never to hurt my son again. Babies are like angels. They need affection. They do not belong to the mature world of elders, nor do they understand the problems of grown-ups.

Vikram, the little chubby child, who used to wear my shoes and put on my sola hat, started avoiding me and even stopped his gibberish singing. He just followed his mother, the kindest woman I know. I felt guilty about the ugly incident, and even to this day, I feel guilty. Of course, the baby had forgotten the cruel incident and was himself again. He loved tram cars and was fascinated when he rode in them. In the first week of every month, I used to go to Bhawanipur Market to buy provisions for the month, as instructed by my wife. My wife suggested I take the baby boy with me, so he could ride the tram. I picked him up in my arms and off we went.

I have always been absentminded, like the professor, who kissed the cat and pushed his wife out of the bedroom, and closed the door behind him. I was given clear instructions about the bag I was to carry, where the money was and to take my son along, when I went shopping. She reminded me to take care of the boy, as he was getting naughty. Vikram, in his impatience, wanted to run down to enjoy the ride in the tram car. I understood his excitement and holding his hand we both set forth to buy the provisions.

The market was a twenty five minute journey away, so after an hour and a half, I returned with all the purchases and accounted for all the money, giving the full account to my wife. She suddenly asked, "Where is Bitto (Vikram)?"

"Oh God!" I suddenly remembered I had taken the baby with me to the market. After the purchases, in the crowded market, I had totally forgotten my son. I now remembered, I had placed him near a heap of rice. I became nervous with fear and anxiety, my wife became hysterical. She started wailing and I went running back to the market.

The twenty five minute journey by tram appeared like a transcontinental crossing. I went from shop to shop, searching for my child. I heard a giggle and lo and behold, it was Vikram, seated near the shopkeeper's cash box, playing with the coins. The shopkeeper scolded me for my carelessness and handed over the baby to me. I picked him lovingly in my arms, and with tears of joy, rushed to catch the first tram home. The tram was not full and as we seated ourselves, a stout, busty, Bengali beauty entered the compartment and occupied the seat just opposite us. Soon, everyone was staring at the open cleavage of her blouse and her royal assets. I thought she was the centre of attraction only for the adult males travelling with us. Little did I know that little Vikram had already pointed his finger at the new attraction. He had learned one very important word and mastered it: "Mamma" (breasts) — and he used it whenever he felt hungry. The openness of the cleavage and the abundant protrusion made Vikram repeat, "Mamma", "Mamma", "Mamma".... till I had to tell him, "Wait, till we get home." The plunging cleavage now became the bare necessity for my boy. Luckily, at the next stop, the lady got down and the jolting journey in the tram car put my son to sleep, while sucking his tiny thumb. On reaching home I handed him over to his anxious mother, shedding tears, and I lovingly kissed his feet, much to the surprise of the baby who wondered what was happening that day.

The doorbell rang, and when I opened it, I found it was Mr. Prithviraj, who wanted me to accompany him to his house, because Debaki Bose was coming to his house for a cup of tea. We would be able to catch up with the latest goings – on in the industry.

One day Mr. Sircar called me and reminded me of what I had said once, "Give me the pen and take away my brush and I shall prove my worth." This is what had prompted him to choose me to write dialogue and songs for the Hindi version of *Devdas*. I thanked them. Some years later he jokingly remarked, "I hope you are not ignoring your homework." When I gave him a puzzled look, he smiled and said, "How many additions are there in the Kidar family, now?" I replied, with a smile too, "I have a son called Vikram and a very naughty daughter called, Prabha. And one more baby is due before Christmas. If he is a boy, he will be called, Birbal. And if it is a girl, she will be named, Gowri or Durga." In those days there was no family planning, but I knew I would not be able to afford more than three children and I have kept that promise.

The innovation, called play back was unknown in the early days of film, and songs had to be recorded directly, along with the camera running. Singers had to start and finish the songs in one go; flowers, clouds, sunsets, etc. were added later. So, only the stars who could sing, were in great demand. Stars like, Mr. K.L. Saigal and Miss Kannan Devi.

Once, during a night shooting, in a jungle behind the studio compound, Umashashi was singing. She was made to stand against a tree laden with flowers. The camera was on a trolley and since it was a direct take, the music director, Mr. R.C. Boral, had no choice but to place the musicians in a pond, where the tree, with the yellow flowers, was growing on the edge. Pictorially, the location was excellent, but for the music director and the musicians, the sound engineer and boom-man, it was a problem.

Mr. Boral ordered his musicians to lift their dhoties and pajamas so that they could enter the pond and stand in it, knee-deep. For the players, who played the flute or the clarinet, it was cozy. But, the musicians who had to play the tabla or the harmonium, had their instruments tied to their waists, and so had to be extra careful. The musicians ignored the cold water and did their best to satisfy Mr. Boral.

Ali Hussain played the tabla. The camera began to roll, the singer started singing and acting, everyone was silent, the director gave cues by signalling, and R.C. Boral conducted the music. Everything was going splendidly till the last couplet where Umashashi started singing the slow and sad part of the song. When all of a sudden Ali Hussain picked up the tempo and doubled the speed of the rhythm, making it four times faster, adding to the anxiety, frustration and anger of the Music Director. The singer completed the song, the Director was happy with the take, but Mr. Boral was furious. Ali Hussain was the first to spring out of the water and when Mr. Boral confronted him saying. "Why did you accelerate the beat when the song required it to be in a slow tempo?" Ali Hussain responded. "Sir, a small fish got into my pajamas and started tickling me. I tried to stay calm but the tickling persisted and I lost concentration and my fingers automatically synchronized with the movements of the fish as it wiggled inside my pajama faster and faster."

One day my landlord informed me that he was going with his family to visit the Greatest Indian poet, the Nobel Laureate, Gurudev Rabindranath Tagore.

I had just finished writing my first book of poems entitled *Punchi* (The Bird). I thought if the great poet Mr. Tagore could just touch my humble work and bless it, I would be thrilled. I had always craved to meet him. I had read the English version of his poems and short stories and was overwhelmed by his penmanship. I implored my landlord to include me with his family and to take me along. The landlord said. "But what should I say if anyone asks me who you are?" I replied. "Just say that I am a domestic servant from Punjab, who loves Shri Tagore's poetry." He agreed and asked me to be ready at the gate the next morning at 7:30 sharp. He then asked if my wife would be accompanying me. "No," I replied "I do not want to bother her because she has work at home, and besides she has children to look after. I have washed, dried my own clothes so as not to disturb her early in the morning."

The next day we left together for Tagore Palace which was quite some distance away. When we reached there I could see from a distance the sage-like figure with his silver white beard. He looked like a picture of 'divine dignity' seated on a cushioned platform with colourful pillows around him. He wore a garland of flowers and the scent of *Agarbatti* (incense) wafted through the air. His devotees were seated on a carpet before him, looking at him with reverence. We all marched into the hall, and when Mr. Banerji's family with myself in tow reached the great Guru, Shri Tagore extended his foot forward and one by one they all kissed it and sat down on the carpet. When I reached him I hesitated and did not want to kiss his foot, so I merely folded my hands in a reverent show of respect and said, "Sire, hopefully you are my future, and I am your past, we need no such formality of my lips kissing your foot."

Everyone was stunned by my impertinence, except Tagore himself. He smiled and offered me a seat on the platform where he was sitting and said "Sit down son, what brings you here?" "The desire to have your *darshan* (audience) and to get your blessings. I have written a book of poems, called Punchi. Here is the manuscript. I would also like to draw a sketch of you on the last page and if you could autograph it and bless it I shall be grateful to you Sir."

He looked at me with a sparkle in his eyes and in a low sweet honey-like voice said. "I am impressed with your honesty and your ego, which makes you quite different from the rest of the crowd. Please recite a line or so from your collection and translate it for me into English, because I do not understand Hindi well." I obeyed and read him a poem and then proceeded to sketch his portrait on the last page of my manuscript. He took the book and signed it with the words, "Blessings."

Then he said that he too had written about a bird, and asked if I would like to listen to the song. This amazed everybody present because Gurudev would not sing even for Kings or princes, but only when his artistic soul felt like singing, like a cuckoo that soars in the boundless sky. And, believe it or not, in a melodious low voice the sage sang for an ugly duckling like me, from his book of verse *Pakhi* The poem "Deen galo amar sonaar khanchar". In this poem there is a line that proves how far Gurudev was ahead of any of us attempting poetry. The gist of the line was 'One day the captive bird, in his lonely cage, saw the Shadow of a free flying bird enter the cage, and he thought he had company. But alas the Shadow soon vanished and did not give the prisoner the opportunity to narrate his sad story' That was a very great day in my life, it was the 25th of March 1938.

Chapter 10

"What I like in a good author is not what he says,

but what he whispers."

Lloyd Logan Smith

Barring a few big guns, who owned cars, the rest of us travelled by tram, being both economical and convenient modes of transportation. Among the big stars Umashashi, K.L.Saigal, and Pahari Sanyal had cars. Nawab Kashmiri travelled by tram and Prithviraj had his bicycle. He had now shifted to a much bigger flat at Bhowanipore, about four miles away from the studio. I was one of those who walked to and from the studio, returning home around 5 pm. when there was no shooting. Prithviraj, who was my buddy, daily walked with me up to my residence, pulling his bicycle along, we would then stop under a lamp-post across my house and keep talking till it got dark. He would then light the bicycle lamp, and ride home whistling. The incident I am about to relate may sound like fiction, but is absolutely true and did happen exactly as I am narrating.

One evening, as usual, my dear friend Prithviraj and me, walked up to the lamp-post, and stood there, engrossed in some discussion. After about half an hour, around 6 pm., Mr. B.N. Sircar our admirable boss was driving by to his house. We both greeted him, and he smiled and nodded back at us, as the car went by.

Soon, the two of us were lost in some kind of profound discussion on Urdu poetry. Prithvi was fond of talking. I too, did not lack in this art. Surprisingly, Prithvi loved to hear me recite Urdu poetry or narrate some engrossing short story – or even crack some smutty jokes. Actually, he just loved my company, this is what Mrs. Prithviraj complained about. That night Prithvi did not light his bicycle lamp, nor did I move away to my flat. The whole night we were engrossed in our conversation. We, two good friends, stood at that very spot, the whole night.

Next morning, when by 9.30 Mr. B.N. Sircar again passed us, on his way to the studio, he was amazed to find us both standing under the same lamp-post, in the same position, talking to each other. He stopped his car and inquired, "Did you two go home last night or have you been standing here the whole night?" That's when it literally dawned on us that we had been standing there, without food or water or sleep, for 16 hours!

The other funny incident, which I can't forget, is travelling with Nawab Kashmiri, to Dharamtulla in a tram car during the filming of *Karorpati*. That day, Nawab Kashmiri was told by the director Hem Chandra, that his performance, as an irritated manager, was lifeless and insipid. Since I had written the dialogue and songs of *Karorpati*, Nawab asked me for my comments. I told him, "To me, you were quite good. But the director has the final say. " Nawab Kashmiri was a very sensitive actor, and he wanted to prove that he was quite good in the scene where he had to snap at his subordinate.

When we were both travelling by the tram car to Dharamtulla, from Tollygunj and the tram car had moved some distance, the conductor, as usual extended his hand and wanted Nawab to pay his fare. Nawab was still lost in the scene, in which he had failed to act properly. He got up from his seat and repeated the lines from the scene, to impress me. He said, "Get out and don't show your face. I said get lost or I shall smash your skull, you scoundrel." The conductor was so flabbergasted that he pulled the chain and asked the driver to stop the tram car at once. The tram car came to a halt, the occupants were shocked to see so much fire and fury in Nawab Kashmiri. The conductor was trembling with fear. Then, Nawab took out some money and paid it to the nervous conductor, saying calmly, "Two tickets to Dharamtulla, please. I am an actor, and I was just rehearsing my lines. My director said I was no good." He turned to the other passengers, "May I have your opinion?" Everyone applauded and clapped, Nawab Kashmiri looked at me and said. "Please tell Hem Chander about my performance." He then pulled out a five-rupee note from his pocket and gave it to the frightened conductor, as *bakshish*, and said, "Your reaction was perfect. Why don't you join the films?" The conductor just ignored Nawab Kashmiri.

Nawab Kashmiri was the same actor who had all his teeth pulled out, just for realism, to play the role of Yahoodi in '*Yahoodi ki Ladki*'. At one time, movies had such wonderful stars, who got so completely involved in their work.

Alam Arzu Lakhanavi was a very renowned Urdu poet of that period. But man cannot live by fame alone. So, to survive, he had came to Calcutta to join New Theatres as a song writer. He was a remarkable old man, very gentle and meek, soft-spoken and warm. I do not know why, but he had some special fascination for me. He enjoyed my company and the lyrics written by me. He valued my opinion on film songs. One of his outstanding numbers was *"Karoon kya aas niras bhaiye...."*

Whenever he wrote a song for a given situation, before submitting it to the director, he would first ask me for my opinion and then hand over the song to the music director. Once Arzu Sahib read the song he had written for Mr. Nitin Bose, to me, for my opinion. Knowing full well that Alama Arzu was an authority on the language, I pointed out that a certain word was wrongly used by him. His response was great, instead of arguing about the correction, he just put a line under the word and said he would think of some other, alternative expression.

That evening when I reached home, I took out the collection of Ghalib's poems and was shocked to find that Ghalib had also used the same word in exactly the manner in which Mr. Arzu had used in his song. I felt very ashamed of my shallow knowledge and my impertinence to tell a great poet, of Alam Arzu's calibre that he had used a certain word wrongly. I immediately rushed to Mr. Arzu's home. His home was situated at Mutiaburj, several miles away. I had to change the tram thrice, and eventually reached quite late at night. When I finally got to Mr. Arzu's house and knocked at the door, he came and opened it amazed to find me there. He looked at me and inquired, "I hope all is well. Your coming to my house at this hour makes me ask this question." While taking my seat near him, I told him that I was very ashamed of my comment, in the afternoon. The word that he had underlined was 100% right and I was totally wrong. I had discovered this while reading Ghalib's poems, so I had come all the way to apologize. Without a further word of any kind, Mr. Arzu went inside, spread the musslah, the carpet for Namaz, and offered his prayers with the zeal of a devotee. The emotionally surcharged Mr. Arzu then came out and embracing me with tearful eyes said, "I want to say many things, but… I do not find words to express myself. I just prayed to the Almighty to give you guidance." He added, "Mr. Sharma, kindly oblige me by accepting a cup of tea from me." I said, "Yes, sir, a cup of tea with extra sugar and more milk, if you do not mind." He said, "Mind? I am delighted to find my honourable guest coming all the way from Tollygunj to Mutiaburj."

During this period, I wrote for films like '*Anaath Aashram*', and '*Zindagi*'. Some of my songs really clicked. K.L.Saigal, is remembered for his rendering of "*Deewana hoon, deewana hoon, rahatt say main baygaana hoon* " and "*Main kya jaanu kya jaadu hai, inn doo mutwaale nainon main jaadu hai, jaadu hai.*" I had also written a lullaby, especially, for my loving wife Raj Dulari.

"So jaa raj dulari so jaa, so jaa main bulhari so jaa." Saigal fell in love with the song, and put immense pressure on me to offer it to the public. Finally my wife agreed, and it was altered to *"So jaa rajkumari so jaa."* Combined with Saigal's wonderful singing, it became a super-hit, and I have long been applauded for it.

When Mr. D.K. Bose came back from Bombay to direct his most ambitious movie, *Vidyapati*, in Hindi and Bengali, Mr. Sircar suggested my name and Mr. Arzu's to be assigned the job of writing the dialogue and lyrics of the Hindi version. He told Mr. Bose, "The choice is entirely yours. I am only suggesting the names of these two very competent writers, for a subject like this." Mr. Bose replied, "Give me a day, Mr. Sircar, and I shall tell you about my choice tomorrow."

Next day, Mr. Bose, who had once refused to give me a small increment of Rs. 5, called me and said, "Kidar, I want you to write the songs and dialogue for *Vidyapati*, and I expect the best from you. Remember, the writer for the Bengali version is none other than Kazi Nazur-Ul-Islam." I thanked him for the honor and I assured him, "I shall do my best and the original poems of the great kavi *Vidyapati* I shall not only translate, but shall render them in Hindi, making them sound like the original. That liberty has to be given to me." Mr. Bose said, "You will have the liberty to some extent, but I shall have the final decision before it goes to Mr. Boral for the music." The script was ready and the shooting of *Vidyapati* started in right earnest.

Pahari Sanyal played Vidyapati's role in both versions, and Kanan Bala and Chhayadevi played the roles of the poet's devotee and the Queen of Mithila, respectively. The Queen of Mithila had fallen in love with the court poet, Vidyapati, her husband's childhood friend. The King in the Hindi version was played by Prithviraj Kapoor, and in the Bengali version, by Mr. Durga Bannerjee, the most famous stage and screen artist of Bengal.

It was rumoured in the New Theaters, in those days, that the Bengali beauty, Chhayadevi was fascinated by Mr. Bose's personality and adored him from the core of her heart. Mr. Bose was used to such occasional flirtations and adoration by his various heroines. He was very careful and shrewd not to demonstrate any feelings on the sets. But, Chhayadevi was simple, and very romantic.

One night, Mr. Bose was shooting an outdoor scene, in the jungle situated just behind the New Theatres studio. It was convenient to take long cables from the studio to light the scene and make the night scene actually look real, rather than shooting it with the red filters and reflectors. Suddenly something went wrong with the camera and there was a break for about 45 minutes. The unit members were told to have tea in the meanwhile, but remain on location and not go to the studio make-up rooms. While Prithviraj Kapoor and I, told the peon, Daya, to get us two cups of coffee, Chhayadevi and D. K. Bose ordered two cups of strong tea and some buttered toast. Daya went to the studio canteen to fetch the refreshments. Prithvi and I started discussing Ghalib. A few yards away, Chhayadevi spread a mat and asked D.K. to keep her company. Mr. Bose had nothing else to do, so he obliged her and they talked in Bengali about some stage actor. We were all waiting for Daya's return with the refreshments.

The moonlight night, the secluded nook in the wilderness and Mr. Bose made Chhayadevi very romantic. She was heard, repeatedly requesting Mr. Bose, "No, no, you must hold my hand a little longer." Mr. Bose being more circumspect said, "Not here, the entire unit is watching." Ms. Chhayadevi retorted, "Nobody is watching. We are alone. Please, D.K., hold my hand for 10 more minutes." The adamant Mr. Bose whispered, "No, no." Then, like all Bengali girls, she said, "Daya, daya" (have mercy on me). She repeated the word louder and louder, "Daya, Daya, Daya…" From behind a tree, Daya, the peon replied, "Yes, Madam, at your service. What is the problem now? I have brought the tea and the toast, what else do you need?" Prithviraj and I laughed at Daya's remarks. Mr. Bose got up and said, "Nothing, nothing. Just leave the tea cups and the toast and get me some paan. And get lost."

The camera department announced a further delay of 30 minutes. And 30 more minutes had to be spent by us all, idling away our time. Mr. Bose thought it was wiser to leave his leading lady and join his male star. He was hesitant to join Durga Bannerjee, as Mr. Bannerjee was enjoying his whisky, and he used to drink like a fish. So, Mr. Bose came to where Nawab Kashmiri, Prithviraj and I were seated on a big stone. Mr. Bose was a very well-read man and a philosopher. Prithviraj loved asking questions on every subject under the sun. So, Prithviraj asked Mr. Bose how to deal with an embarrassing situation when a sex urge bothers you and you are expected to behave. Mr. Bose thought for a while and then said, "I read a Sanskrit couplet, which I cannot remember now, but the meaning of the couplet is that when you are sexually aroused, the best remedy to control it is a glass of cold water. Drink it and you will be calmed again." Then Nawab asked, "What about *ganne ka ras* (sugar-cane juice)? Mr. Bose frozenly replied, "I don't know about that."

Finally, the cameraman announced that everything was fine and the shot was ready, it was the retake for the Hindi version, a romantic scene between the king and his charming queen. So Chhayadevi and Prithviraj were told to rehearse the shot before the final take. The director also reminded Prithviraj to add fire and desire in his eyes, when he gazed into the eyes of his beloved queen. Just like Durga Bannerjee had done in the Bengali version. Prithviraj promised to do his best, but said no rehearsals were needed, "Please allow me to do a direct take. I know my lines."

Mr. Bose shouted, "Start sound – start camera." Prithviraj in a very romantic tone said, "Oh my beloved, hold my hand a little longer, just a little more (these lines were inserted by him for added effect). I adore you from the core of my heart. Then Chhayadevi said, "Cut" and asked Daya, the peon," Quick, get me a glass of cold water, Daya, quick." She said it innocently, but Nawab Kashmiri, who was there, could not help langhing. Mr. Bose felt rather embarrassed. When Chhayadevi, after drinking the glass of water, said, "Oh what a relief...I was so hot and I have been thirsty since long." she looked at Mr. Bose for his wise comments.

After a few days, Mr. Bose called me to his office and said, "Here is a very very romantic song, written by Vidyapati, himself, which Anuradha sings, while trying to tease the poet. It is going to be the hit song and I want a word for word translation." I said, "I shall try. Please read me the whole song, word by word, explaining its every poetic nuance and excellence." Mr. Bose recited with all his fervor and enthusiasm the song of Anuradha, who tells the poet *"Aangan aawat jub rasiya, palti chalat hun hasiya"* (when my beloved comes to my courtyard, I shall saunter with a smile and a sway). All was okay, till the part where Anuradha utters these words, *"Kachuwa dharat jub piyara"* (when my lover holds my breast). I became hesitant and humbly interrupted Mr. Bose, suggesting it was not proper for a lady to say such a thing openly, she could be bashful, aesthetic and at the same time suggestive. This made Mr. Bose furious, and he told me he was using the original song from Vidyapati for the Bengali version, so why would the Hindi audience find it objectionable or offensive? My reply was, "Sir, this is a matter of attitude and culture. So far as culture and tradition go, some of the Hindi audience would likely call it obscene and in poor taste. Anuradha is shown complaining, and even perhaps, complimenting her lover, and the great poet holds her breasts! May I, with your permission, repeat an old English saying to illustrate my point?" Mr. Bose, angrily retorted, "Yes, you may." Then I told him, they say that when a lady says "no", she means, "perhaps" – and when she says "perhaps", she hints "oh, yes." But when she says "yes", she is no lady. Therefore, since Anuradha is not a cheap girl, I suggested she should use a more subtle expression. Mr. Bose was very sarcastic and said, "Can you improve upon Vidyapati's original writing, providing a different expression." And I said, "Of course, but I need time."

I was given two days and on the third day I completed the song. Keeping all the other lines exactly as written by Vidyapati, himself, except this line, when she speaks about her lover holding her breasts. In my version Anuradha says, *"Choli pay nazariya jaye, mori chunari lipat mose jaaye"*, (when his glance rivets on my blouse, my dupatta (veil) will hide my embarrassment). It was in the song starting thus: *"More aangana main aaye aali main chaal chalun mutwali,"* and was beautifully sung by Kanan Devi.

Mr. R.C. Boral said, "Hats off to Kidar for writing such a wonderful line and such a beautiful song. I shall now compose a very fine tune, too." Mr. Bose also said, "You have provided a good substitute. As a director, to show Anuradha's bosom, I need an insertion of the close-up and the line of the song allows me to express it in an artistic manner."

It was a practice with Mr. Bose, as well as other Bengali directors, to shoot the Bengali version first. When the Bengali actors were rehearsing, the Hindi stars like Prithvi, Nawab or Saigal, were asked to watch carefully and then reproduce the same kind of performance to perfection. Only then were the Hindi versions of that particular shot taken.

Every time Mr. Bose instructed Prithviraj to watch carefully the loud gestures of Durga Bannerjee, Prithviraj, felt humiliated but being a thorough gentleman, would always politely say, "I am watching carefully, but please allow me to sometimes use my own acting talents. I have had my training under the very renowned director of the English stage, Grant Anderson, who came from London." Mr. Bose did not argue, but insisted that the Hindi players copy the Bengali actors.

When the film was nearing completion, and the climax scene was being shot, in which Rani Laxman had decided to commit suicide by taking poison, before going to the temple to die at the feet of the Lord, someone had to come rushing in to inform the King about the Queen's intentions. As usual the Bengali shot was taken first. Durga Bannerjee, the King, when informed about this tragic news, instead of rushing to his beloved queen, spent quite a lot of time telling those around him, how silly the fair sex was, and gave a long lecture, before leaving for the temple, to save his dying beloved. After the take, everyone on the set clapped and applauded Durga Babu's excellent performance. In the Hindi version, the King, Prithviraj, just showed shock and dismay, and only said, "*Sarva naash, hey Bhagwan meri laaj rakhna*" (all is lost, Lord be my savior), and rushes out of the palace, like a man possessed.

Mr. Bose told him it was a very insipid shot. Prithviraj argued that the dialogue writer had only given him these two lines, so what was he supposed to do? Mr. Bose beckoned me and asked why I had not given Prithviraj lines similar to those spoken by Durga Bannerjee. My reply was, "The Queen is about to take poison, she is planning to die alone in the temple, then why should the King, her loving husband, waste time repeating words of wisdom and deliver a long sermon, when he should be rushing to the temple to save his beloved

Queen?" There was pin-drop silence. Prithvi was the first to speak,"His argument is correct, he is right. Urgency demands that the King should rush immediately to the Queen." And I added, "The long lecture about the silly nature of the fair sex can await a more appropriate moment." This made Mr. Bose flare up and he shouted, "Have I to learn direction from you two Punjabis? This is sheer impertinence. I, D.K. Bose, as the captain of the unit, order everyone to pack up. I cannot be insulted like this by a mere dialogue writer and his actor buddy."

All the Bengalis present were supportive of Mr. Bose and said, "Mr. B.N. Sircar must be told to punish this rude young man, a painter pretending to be a writer – these Punjabis are swollen headed." The biggest crime in films is to cause a 'pack-up' and a stoppage of work. The offenders are always dealt with severely. So, that day I was the criminal and I awaited punishment. Everyone left the set in a jiffy, except Prithviraj and myself, both crestfallen, both loyal workers. My main concern was not the probability of losing the good job I had, but having to face Mr. B.N. Sircar, my benefactor and the Big Boss of New Theatres, who had made me a writer against all opposition. That night I did not sleep a wink.

The next morning I went to the studio. Mr. Bose had resumed shooting and there was no reference at all to the previous day's ugly incident. I was very surprised. I could imagine that Mr. Sircar must have heard about the entire argument from Mr. Bose and the other supporters, who lodged a complaint against the two Punjabis. He must have asked what Prithvi and Kidar had to say, and when told about our remarks, must have said, "Gentlemen, this is honesty and not ego of Kidar and Prithvi. Since the Queen was planning to die, the King must rush to the temple to save her. My advice is to resume shooting and complete the sequence. And also, forget and forgive."

Mr. Sircar was a very big-hearted boss. He often gave judgments that surprised everybody. For instance, once, a poor boom boy was somewhat nice to an extra girl, who was sick and for whom he brought lunch, during the break, from the canteen. This gesture of his was wrongly presented to Mr. Sircar. The latter sarcastically said, "When the heroine is served by the director or the music director, you angels never come to complain to me. Why?" With their heads bent low, the three 'angels' walked away. That was Mr. B.N. Sircar's kind of justice.

Jagdish Sethi introduced me to a newcomer, Romola, who was working on stage, and recommended her for some roles in the films. She was smart and a charming young lady. Her only drawback was her height. She was not tall, but she had lofty ambitions. One day she came to see me and I promised I would personally take her to the director of her choice. She said, "I would like to be introduced to Mr. Nitin Bose, and no one else." I took her to Mr. Bose, and was sure that her charm and talent would impress him.

Mr. Bose scanned her, from top to toe, while I praised her talent and her choice of a directo, like Nitin Bose. After a long silence, Mr. Bose addressed me and said, "When you brought her to me, why did you forget to bring some bricks

I have had my share of awards and rewards.The awards include a Unesco Award, Indian Film Directors' Associations Lifetime Achievement Award, A Gold Award from Prime Minister Indra Gandhi in 1982 for contribution to Indian Cinema, The Shantaram Award, and The Venice Film Festival Award. My rewards are however more important because they are a collection of people and memories. People that I have met and befriended, memories that I have cherished. From great statesmen like Nehru to emanant poets like Gurudev Tagore. I know that I have indeed walked amongst giants and hope that I too will perhaps leave behind a small footprint in the sands of time.

(Ironically Kidar Sharma was to handed one more award. It was the Raj Kapoor Award, an award named after his deciple to be given to the Guru.)

Romola and my sketch of B.N. Sircar, who was the boss of New Theatres.

On the sets of *Jhanjhar* with Kamani Kaushal and my Guru, Bose when he visited me. I have never stopped shooting even when the most important visitors came on my set. He of course, was an exception.

When I returned from Singapore I was once again forced to make my own movies to survive. This time I made *Hamari Yaad Aayegi* with my son Ashok (Billy) and Tanuja. The main song of the movie became an instant hit.

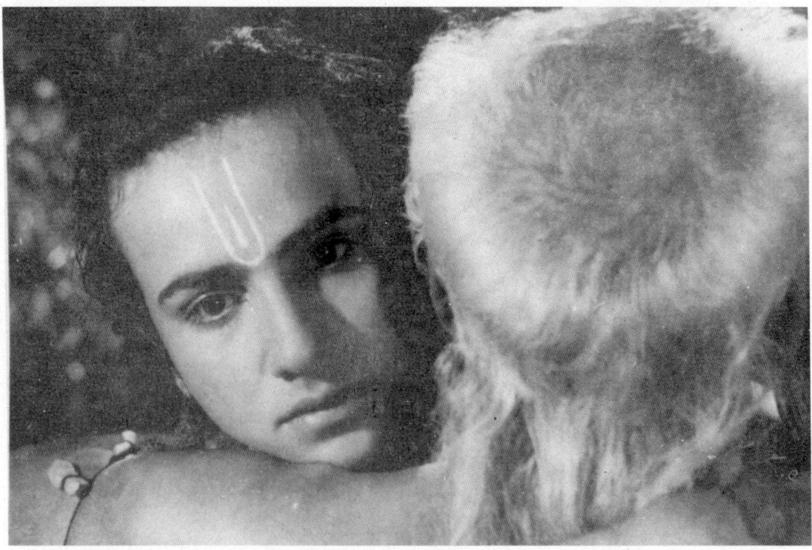

I made several movies for the Children's Film Society. But my first movie *Jaldeep* and my last movie *Ganga Ke Lahren* was with my son Ashok (Billy) were memorable.

With Ashok Kumar

On the set of my film *Aulad*, when I got my first chance to write and direct a movie. I am seated 2nd. from left in the front row. Gyani is standing next to me while Romola is directly above him.

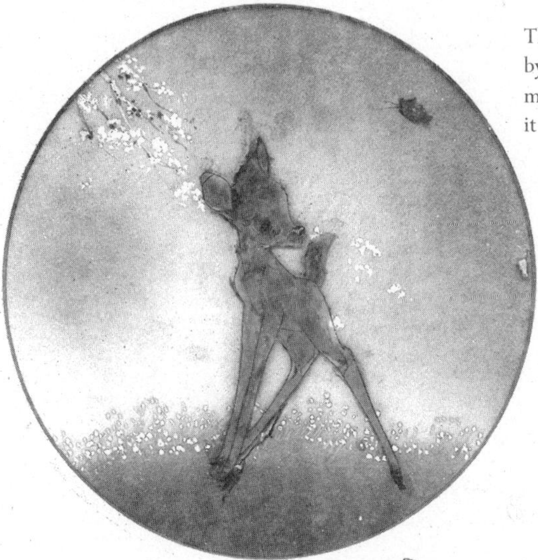

This frame fro Bambi.autographed by Walt Disney is very precious to me. This creative genius and I hit it off very well.

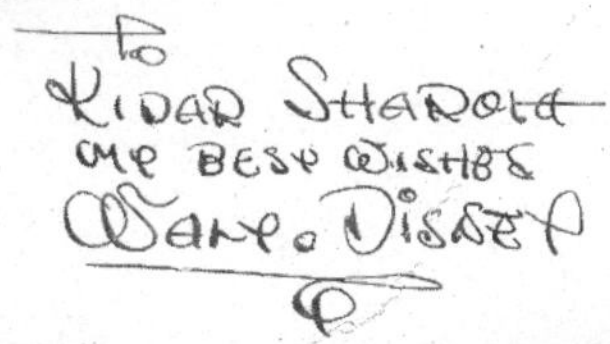

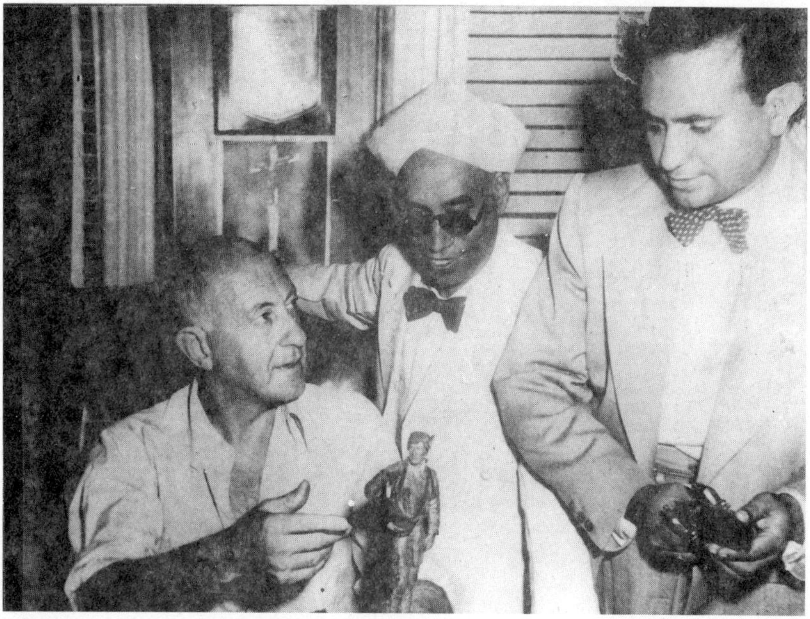

The Great Cecil B. De Mille explaining his approach to the making of *The Ten Commandments.*

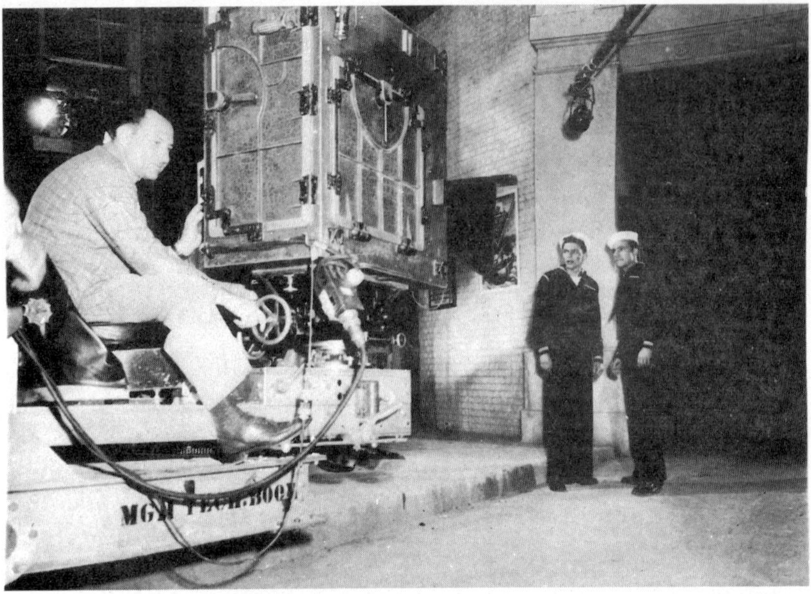

Frank Sinatra and Gene Kelly in the movie *On the Town*

With Glassberg, who was the Chief Cinematographer at MGM at that time. He became my friend and guide.

Four of us as part of the Indian Delegation, Sundar Rajan, Hirlekar, myself and Shorey. We were taken to the sets of every major motion picture. In Hollywood I met my idols Charlie Chaplin, Gary Cooper, Frank Capra, Ray Milland, Walt Disney and Cecil B. DeMille. I was impressed by them all. Especially the work ethics of actors like Ray Milland who would show up as early as 6.00 a.m. to rehearse his part in *The Lost Weekend*. He won an Oscar.

In 1945, I was chosen to go to England and Hollywood as part of thet first Indian Film Delegation. This was during the war which was raging at its height in Europe .

This beautiful statue adorned the lobby of the Waldorf Astoria hotel. I was so fascinated by this statue that although it was forbidden to photograph it during the war, I just had to capture it on film. So I hid my camera in a shoe box and got the perfect picture.

opp pg
▲ Every actor from the big stars like Gyani, and Mehtab to even smaller charecters like Ram Dulari had all put in a super performance in the movie, *Chitralekha.*

▶ *Shoikhiyan* starred the two big names in those days. Suraiya and Premnath. It was a historical movie which depicted how the Portuguese gained access to India.

▲ ▶ Stills from the movie *Chitralekha.* Which became an all time hit. The movie was hailed as a masterpiece for it's writing, direction, photography, set decoration, art direction and the powerful performances by its main stars.

The costumes and the set decor were so lavish that in those days it rivaled even the biggest Hollywood film, and yet it was produced on a very small budget. It took me months to draw hundreds of sketches covering every small detail.

Two of my closest friends have been K.L. Saigal (above) and Prithviraj Kapoor (opp pg) Both were legends in their time.

Saigal had two passions - Music and Alcohol. One made him, the other destroyed him. There are many stories about his greateness as a singer and actor, but the ones that will always stay in my memory are those of him as a humane, gracious giver.

◀

During my initial attempt to get into movie; three people were most helpful. The first was Durga Khote, who introduced me to D.K. Bose.The other two were K.L. Saigal and Prithviraj. I shall always be indebted to all three of them for accepting me so openly. Finally, I owe a lot to my Guru, D.K. Bose for sensing a spark in me and taking me under his wing.

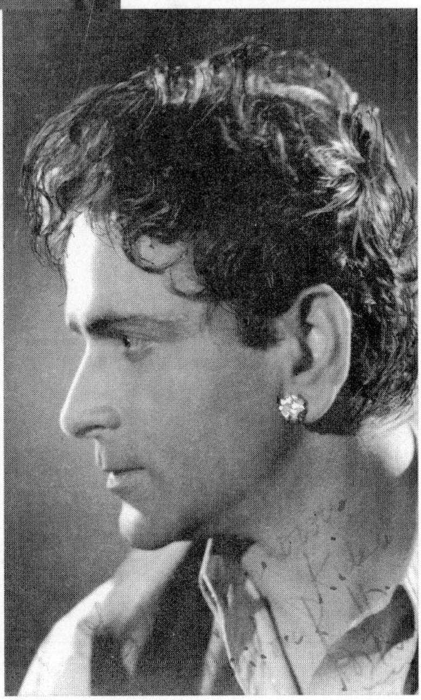

▶

Prithviraj loved theater and literature and was always like a brother to me. He gave so much to the Indian film industry. Yet his most enduring gift to films has been the incredible pool of talent his family members have contributed from generation to generation, thus keeping the Kapoor name shinning.

During the mahurat of *Chetak* with Prithviraj. Both Kamani Kaushal and Kishore Kumar attended.

Prithviraj made *Chetak* with me. He played Maharana (King) Pratap. In one scene the king's faithful horse Chetak gets wounded,but before the horse dies, the King sensing his horse's pain places his cheek on the dying horse's cheek to comfort and silently speak to his beloved companion.

Years later when Prithviraj was sick in hospital I went to meet him. He knew how seriously ill he was. He asked me place my cheek on his. He passed away soon after that.

◀

It was the picture of my friend, the dashing and handsome Prithviraj as a king. Someone had tampered with the original negatives that I had taken during the filming of the movie.

I was invited to Singapore to make films. In my first and last foreign film for Shaw Brothers called *Kaka Kura*. I worked with a chinese crew. The film was shot in Mandarin. On the set of the movie with my staff of writers.
Filming outdoors with a great crew. I enjoyed my work there and was treated very well abroad. However destiny had other plans for me and I decided to return to India.

for her to stand on?" Poor Romola was hurt and heart-broken by this great director's caustic remark. She quietly said, "Goodbye" and walked away from his office.

I followed her and found that she was in tears. I was moved by the plight of a struggling youngster having high hopes, being ridiculed for something which nature was responsible for. I knew what it felt like to be ridiculed. I had experienced it often enough. I escorted her to the tram junction and there she bid me goodbye. To encourage her, I said, "Please, Romola, don't be heart-broken. One day, when I become a director, you will be my first heroine, and we will prove to Mr. Bose and the world, what a great star you are." Romola laughed and said, "Poor Mr. Kidarnath, the dialogue-writer will never be a director and I will never be a heroine." So saying, she jumped into the tram.

Vidyapati was coming to an end. One day, during an interval in the shooting, the important stars had gone to the make-up room to change their costumes. Mr. Bose was chatting with the cameraman and the sound engineer, and had left his file of the scenario on his table. God knows why, I picked up the file and casually started glancing through it. Being the dialogue writer and the lyricist of the movie, I felt I was an important member of Mr. Bose's unit, so there was no harm in studying the script, written by the head of the unit. I had hardly gone through a page, when the file was rudely snatched from my hand. It was the assistant director. I wanted to complain to Mr. Bose about this rude behaviour. But to my surprise I was judged as the guilty party. Mr. Bose, in a rage, demanded, "How dare you touch that file? And with whose permission were you studying it?" I could only utter two words, "Sorry, Sir."

But the matter did not end there. I was court-marshalled for touching the scenario, and being a non-Bengali, that was a crime! As a result of this humiliation, I decided to become a director. A director, who would teach, groom and inspire youngsters to learn the art. How could a tree survive, if the flowers are not allowed to bloom? Cinema, for its growth, must permit new talent to grow. In those days, there were no film institutions and you had the *Guru-Shishya parampara* (teacher-pupil tradition). The day Vidyapati's shooting finished, I decided to leave New Theatres and become a film director. This was an unwise, stupid and dangerous move, but I had to take the risk and the challenges, something that I had learned from my childhood.

I confided in my friend Prithviraj, who said, "Next Monday, I too shall give you a surprise." Next Monday meant waiting for five days more. When Monday came, Prithviraj told me, "I have resigned from New Theatres, today. When Kidar Sharma leaves, how can I stay behind? I am going back to Bombay and God will provide me a job and daily meals for me and my family." I was touched by the affection and loyalty of my friend, Prithviraj. We both left New Theatres, after the completion of *Vidyapati*, and everyone thought we were foolish and stupid.

Chapter 11

"Pawon say lipti huye hai koocha-e-jaana ki khaak, jaane kub say zairay pa munzil leeiya phirrta hun main."

(The clay of my beloved's abode is clinging to my feet, How long have I been carrying my Goal and Destiny underfoot?)

One of my favourite couplets, written by my younger brother, Himmat Rai.

I fixed a signboard on the door of my flat, with the words, 'Kidar Sharma -Director'. I had dropped 'Nath' from my name, to make it sound more crisp and important.

With Prithviraj having left for Bombay, I had to face some trying times. My wife said, "By simply adding the title, 'director', to your name, you have denied yourself any chance of being asked to write dialogue or songs." And then she added, "You keep sitting idle at home. Who do you think you are going to direct?" My reply was, "I direct you, my loving wife, and don't discourage me now, when you have always stood by me. Don't feel sorry for me or advise me. I have travelled a long way to attain my goal. I have my dreams and I will become a dream-merchant one day." She whispered, "Best of luck."

Gradually, my savings began to dwindle and once again I had to face some hard times. I was unemployed in a big city, I had a big flat and three small children to look after in Calcutta, and to support my parents in Punjab. In those days, K.N. Singh was my guest. I had five rooms, so I gave him one large room. He had come to Calcutta to join films. When K.N. Singh found out that I had no job but was too proud to accept money, he very gracefully arranged some other accommodation and left with a smile and a thank you.

Troubles never come alone. My three kids fell sick and had high fever. My elder son, Vikram, was a born philosopher, and told me one day, "When naughty children get no spanking from their loving parents for their mischief, God punishes them with high fever and a bad throat." My little daughter, Prabha, when she heard what he had said about naughty children said, "Dad, I have a confession to make. I was naughty, too, I stole the full tin of Ovaltine. I gave very little to Bitto and Billy, but I ate the whole tin myself. Now that I have confessed and have asked for forgiveness, I am sure that we three naughty children are going to be okay tomorrow. Please tell Mummy not to cry. I know she is very sad and weeps alone, all the time."

Surprisingly, both Vikram and Prabha had no temperature the next day. But my youngest son, my favourite, was still shivering with high fever. I could not afford a doctor's fee, for his visit. I could not even afford a rickshaw to take the sick child to a doctor, who was half a mile away. My wife gave me Rs.5 and begged me to take Billy to the doctor, the next morning. I wrapped the child in a blanket and started walking down the road. Then I noticed a truck from the New Theatres coming down the road with a load of furniture. I stopped the truck. The driver knew me. I requested him to give me and my sick child a lift up to the next bridge, as a thunderstorm was approaching and it was going to rain. I had no umbrella even then. The truck-driver rudely refused to give me a lift, saying, "You have left New Theatres. I can't give you a lift. Hire a rickshaw." Then he drove away.

It started raining heavily. I ran for shelter, carrying my sick child and stood under a big tree. There was no rickshaw in sight. I couldn't even go home. I was sad and on the verge of tears. My youngest son, Billy, whom I call my heart, heard my heartbeats and whispered, "Do not be sad, Dad. A person like you should travel in his own car and not in that lousy truck, driven by the nasty driver. Let me get well and we will buy a green car and travel together in our own car. Okay? Now smile Dad."

Thank God, the rain stopped. I took Billy to the doctor, a Mr. Dass Babu, who was a famous homeopath. He said, "The child will need ten days to recover. Here is some medicine for two weeks. There is no cause to worry. I have checked him and he is tough. Touch wood." After Dass Babu gave me the medicine, I quietly put the five rupee note on the table, saying, "I am sorry, I have only five rupees to offer. I shall pay the balance, next time, I promise."

Dass Babu looked at me and replied, "What balance? Homeopathic medicine does not cost much and I don't practice to amass wealth. I do it to serve humanity. Here, I am returning two rupees and the medicine only costs Rs. 3. Take the child home in a rickshaw, because the weather is nasty."

Then, turning to Billy, the doctor said, "What would you like to be when you grow up, son? A doctor? A policeman? An actor?" Billy replied, "I will be my dad's driver. We are buying a green car, as soon as I get well." The doctor was amused and said, "You have a child just like you. He wants to be a dream merchant, too."

With the two rupees, Billy and I came home in a rickshaw. Billy received the medicine regularly, but showed no signs of any improvement, even after a week! My worries multiplied, but I would not bend. K.L. Saigal, who visited me often, had said, "Please go back to New Theatres and apologize to Mr. Sircar and tell him that you are sorry, and things will be okay again." But I was adamant. He left me alone but he was not annoyed.

When I told the doctor about Billy's condition, he said, "Don't worry, the fever will last for ten days. Your green car can wait for a few days. The child will be okay soon." The doctor's advice gave me some peace of mind but his mother was very worried. She was sorry to see the little boy bed-ridden for so many days.

Being still unemployed, for months, my financial condition deteriorated. I had not paid rent to the landlord for three months. He could easily have thrown me out from such a spacious and economical flat. But he did not.

Suddenly the thought of my grandmother's *Bhajan* (the SOS to God) came to my mind and I hummed it to put Billy to sleep. I had hardly finished singing when the doorbell rang. I thought it was the landlord, who had come with a legal document to collect his rent. I asked my wife to say that I was not at home. And if he asked, to say that he would be paid in a day or so. My wife gave me a look, which said, "You obstinate sufferer, you are doing this for your false ego." To add insult to injury, she remarked, "I will tell him that the director sahib has gone for outdoor shooting and will be back in a day or so." I was hurt and Billy remarked, "See mummy is very intelligent." I said sarcastically, "Yes, son, she is and I am not."

My wife returned and said, "There is a registered letter for you and the postman wants you to sign for it." I thought it was a legal notice from the landlord. But she remarked that it was from Bombay. I was puzzled. Who would send me a registered letter from Bombay?

When I opened the letter, I began to cry with joy. It was from Seth Chandulal Shah of Ranjit Movietone, who had sent me a demand draft of Rs. 7000, saying this was for my story idea of the script of '*Rickshawalla*', which I had given to his director, Mr. Chatrabhuj Doshi, when he visited Calcutta and met me with Mr. Ezra Mir. Mr. Shah liked the storyline and had hired Mr. Mir to direct it.

As I have said, "God is only a whisper away." And my SOS to Bhagwan was heard, once more. We were all happy, and each one touched the demand draft. Billy kissed it and said, "We will buy a green car for Dad." Prabha responded, "...and a tricycle for me and a small car for Bitto."

The next day, Billy's fever was gone. The seven thousand, which was a very big amount in those days, proved to be the tonic. I had never seen so much money in all my life. I deposited the money in my savings account at the Lloyd's Bank and paid the outstanding rent. Vikram said, "I think happy days are here again." And Billy said, "Now that my fever has gone and also our poverty, Dad please take us to the zoo. I would like to see lions, tigers and an elephant. I have never seen an elephant in all my life." My wife, then added, "I have lived in Calcutta for so many years, but I have never seen the Victoria Memorial."

The next Sunday, we visited the zoo and the Victoria Memorial. I cannot forget the joy of my children, poor till yesterday. I bought them every little thing they desired.

I still remember Billy remarking, after seeing the elephant, "This animal is strange. He has a tail attached to his nose." Billy was born with great humour and courage even as a child. He undauntedly ran forward to stroke the huge trunk of the big elephant. His mother shrieked and Bitto rushed to hold Billy back. Prabha started crying. In her childhood, Prabha broke all records for crying. She could cry the loudest and the longest.

Next week, there was another surprise. Mr. M.N. Malhotra, the ace cameraman, and Mr. R.C. Talwar, both foreign-trained technicians, came to see me. Mr. Talwar was once my classmate in Amritsar. They told me that they were sent by the Managing Director of a newly formed company,

The Film Corporation of India, with a message that I must see Mr. Kabra, the Managing Director, for some urgent work. When I inquired about the nature of this urgent work, I was told that the director of a film, '*Tumhari Jeet*', which was under-production, had married an English girl, and had gone to London, leaving the film incomplete. They added, "If you can kindly complete the film, the manager, would feel highly obliged." I thought for a while and said, "I shall come tomorrow to see Mr. Kabra, at 10 o'clock."

My eldest son, who was listening to our conversation, called me into the passage and said, "I told you Dad, happy days are here again, but please show some interest in the job you are being offered." I thanked my philosopher, friend, and guide for his advice. Then the child philosopher said, "Bend down and let me kiss your forehead. You need some luck."

After the visitors had departed, the Sharma family assembled for a conference. They were all so surcharged with the big news that no one could say a word. Then Billy remarked, "Dad, now you can go outdoors for your shooting so that mummy's predictions can come true." And Vikram remarked, "When I grow up, I am not going to marry any woman." Surprisingly the little chap has kept his word. Dr. Vikram Sharma is still a bachelor to this day.

I met Mr. Kabra and I was hired right away. While we talked, the manager Mr. R. Sharma had my contract typed. He offered a lump sum amount of Rs. 3000 for the entire work of finishing the remaining portion of the film. They paid me Rs. 500 cash for signing. Everyone, including Shaukat

Hussain, the young editor, was delighted to have me in their team. When I thanked them, Mr. Sharma retorted, "A jeweller knows the worth of a gem. And yes, Kidar Sharma is a rare gem, which New Theatres never deserved." Before the shooting began, I was told to check with my chief assistant to see the rushes of the already shot film sequences, and to somehow complete the film.

When I went home and told everyone that I had been called a 'gem' and how happy I was to be engaged as a film director, the three kids started dancing. My darling daughter, Prabha, who has a lot of rhythm in her, danced the most. Now that money was not a problem, Billy insisted on the green car and I promised we would get one after the movie was completed.

My brother, Himmat Rai, and my brother-in-law, Rajendra Sharma, had come to stay with me and try their luck in films, too. I had a big flat, so that was not a problem. On the first day of the shooting, I was nervous, but I kept my cool. When I left home, my son Bitto combed my hair and my daughter put a little tilak on my forehead, after some kind of puja. Billy reminded me, "Don't forget to pretend that you are a great director. We have to bring home a green car."

I confess that I can pretend and make others believe that I have great confidence and skill, that I am a master of any situation. But that day, when I reached the studio floor, I had to control my legs from shaking and my heart from beating too fast. My heroine for this film was Miss Chhayadevi, the Queen in *Vidyapati* and the favourite of the great film director, Mr. D.K. Bose, to whom Chhayadevi appeared as a silly stupid woman, but who for the sake of sabhyata called her a simpleton.

Ms. Chhayadevi loved all her directors, big or small, and she assured me of her support with a benevolent smile. I smiled back and said, "I am going to start with a tight close-up." She was puzzled. She had heard of a close-up, but a 'tight' close-up was a real mystery to her.

Mr. Malhotra, my Germany-trained cinematographer, was keen to test my knowledge as a director and asked me, "Which lens should I use for this tight close-up, Sharmaji?" I did not know the correct answer to his question, and I asked, "How many lenses have you got?" He replied, "Four — a 25, a 50, a 75 and a 100." I said, "Let me look at these lenses." The lenses were handed to me.

I picked up each and selected the heaviest, the 100 lens.

Mr. Malhotra said, "I never knew you had so much knowledge about cinematography, too."

Pretending paid off, once again. The art of fibbing has enabled me to become a fiction-writer. And perhaps self-deception alone has helped me to exist, under severe and painful circumstances. *"Baquadre paymanna-e-taqhayul, khummar hur dil main hai khudi ka, agar na ho yeh furraib-e-peham, to dumm nikal jaaye aadmi ka."* (Full to the brim, each one is intoxicated by our ego; without this self deception, man would breathe his last.)

When the film was completed, I made sure that I got the balance of Rs. 2500. During the first trial, Chhayadevi wept and cried like a child. She was so moved with the story, and the tragic scenes, that her copious tears affected the audience reaction to the film quite a lot. The unit members were raving about my skill as a director. My cameraman and the editor asked me to console my heroine, who was still sobbing. So I went and sat near her and asked, "Is the film really so touching?" She said, "Yes." Then I asked her, "Will the audience cry, too, when the film is released?" She said, "Yes, oh Yes." Then I inquired, "What about the critics?" And she replied, "Yes, Yes, Yes." So I asked her jokingly, "Will the producer also cry?" And she replied innocently, "Yes, of course."

When, Mr. R. Sharma joined us, Chhayadevi knowing how important a person he was, started crying again, and asked me for my handkerchief. Since I never had one, Mr. R. Sharma offered her his. She wiped the tears and blew her nose with zeal. How simple this woman really was only God and Chhayadevi knew.

My temporary assignment, to complete this unfinished film, won me great admiration and a great friend. Mr. R. Sharma liked me for my pen and admired me for my honesty, praised me for my sense of humour and my knowledge of music. Since I had completed their film, it was time to say goodbye.

When I went to Mr. Kabra's office, to say goodbye, and ask for the balance of my fee, Mr. Kabra smiled and said, "You are not going to leave the Film Corporation of India. You better see Mr. R. Sharma, collect your cheque and sign a new contract."

I was surprised, and I went to Mr. Sharma, who gave me two cheques, one for the balance for the film, of Rs. 2500 and another cheque of Rs. 1000, as the signing amount for directing two more films for them. The total amount for these two films was Rs. 20,000, to be paid in installments. I was overjoyed. I knew I could complete the two films in a year's time.

A week later, I submitted the script of '*Aulad/ Dil Hi To Hai*' to Mr. Sharma, for his approval. It was the first off-beat film, dealing with human problems. It was neither a mythology nor was it a theatrical Romeo and Juliet venture. After a fortnight, I was told to go ahead and select the stars for my first independent directorial venture. I told Mr. Sharma, "I do not need stars. I need suitable artists and willing workers. Even if they are raw hands. I have the ability to train them, and get the best performance out of them." Mr. Sharma replied, "You have complete freedom and our complete co-operation. But remember, you will also be totally responsible for the results." I said, "I know that." And we parted.

Aulad was the first new-wave film and, therefore, it was like it taking quite a risk. It was not a musical romance nor was it a costume drama, with dazzling sets. It was a down-to-earth story of a middle-class father, who had sacrificed all his life to educate his son and his darling daughter, hoping that they would be worthy children to the society and to the family. Little did the old man know that the generation gap would present a different, horrifying reality, which would destroy him completely. This film had the lines, "*Paon may roundda humay aapno nay baygaanon nay, haath pukra jo musebbat main toe aarmanon nay.*" (I have been trampled on, both by my kin, and those not my own. The only support I got was from hope and wishes.)

I think I felt the need of our nation, which was struggling in those days for freedom. I saw the need to prepare the youth so when freedom was given to them, they would know how to digest it. So that rather than just demanding rights, they would accept responsibility and obligations, too. In my opinion, it was a necessary message, as the leaders had no time for this. And the teachers and thinkers seemed oblivious to it. I thought *Aulad* would give my country a hint about such an important issue. Time proved that freedom comes to those who were qualified enough to make full use of this blessing.

The modern college Miss, who destroys the dreams of her old father, the aged struggling middleclass man, was played by Romola, the same girl whom I had once taken to Mr. Nitin Bose and who was rejected for her short height. I kept my promise that she would be the heroine of my first film. For the main male role I chose Mr. A.S. Gyani, whom I had admired as the star of amateur theatre while I was a student in Amritsar. Unfortunately Mr. Gyani was struggling and working as an extra in Bombay. I contacted him and gave him a chance to star in a film in Calcutta. While Gyani expressed his thankfulness in so many emotional ways, Miss Romola only said, "Thanks." She was more interested in my first assistant, Mr. R.C. Talwar and soon she made him her friend, philosopher and guide. Romola explained, bashfully and truthfully, the meaning of the word, 'guide'. She said, "He is smart. He gets his commission in advance, for rendering his services eventually." R.C. Talwar was a classmate and friend so I ignored his relationship with Romola.

Another remarkable person who I met while making *Aulad* was my music director, Shri Bhissham Dev, a master of his art and a soft-spoken saint. He was an English writer and he once remarked that he wanted to hastily return thither, whence he had come from. He renounced the world soon and became an ascetic.

Since I was financially quite comfortable now, I allowed myself two luxuries. The first was bringing home a green car, a thrill to my youngest son, Billy. My English car was a beauty, it was a green, second-hand Wolsely, with all the dignity that goes with an English car. The second was to shift from 70 Russa Road to an entire building with ground floor, first floor and second floor all for us. I found such a building, next door! The ground floor was given to the boys, my younger brother, Himmat Rai and brother-in-law, Rajendra Sharma, who brought a friend of his from Rawalpindi also to stay with them. His friend, a Sardarji, was meek as a lamb and extremely religious.

I worked very hard to make *Aulad*, an emotional masterpiece, and I did succeed to quite an extent in my endeavor. During its first trial Mr. Dalsukh Pancholi, who had started his own production in Lahore, happened to be there and he made up his mind to take away two of my artists — Gyaniji and Romola — after seeing the audience reaction. He secretly negotiated with them, telling them not to reveal his plans to their director, Kidar Sharma, who had discovered and groomed them. Since loyalty is not a popular practice in show business, both my favourite artists kept Mr. Pancholi's plans a guarded secret from me and Mr. R. Sharma, who had done a lot to establish them as stars. Actually they were nobodies, compared to film stars of those days, like K. L. Saigal, Motilal, Prithviraj, Nawab, Kanan Devi, Umashashi, Leela Desai to name a few.

Another surprise was that *Aulad* was to have it's premiere in Bombay. And that, too, through Shri Reva Shankar Pancholi, the elder brother of Mr. D. Pancholi.

Mr. Reva Shankar, a thorough gentleman, insisted that Pandit Kidar Sharma must attend the release of this off-beat film in Bombay, and discuss the importance of the subject with the Bombay press, for which he would make all the arrangements. So I had to go to Bombay for the release of my first film. Mr. Reva Shankar did not put me up in a hotel. He took me straight to his own home to stay with his family members. He was so loving, so gentle and so honest. I was very young in those days and being of slender build, no one believed that I had directed this off-beat film, packed with sublime sentiment and good directorial touches. *Aulad* was released at the Krishna Cinema, which was quite popular, but since neither the company, which had produced this film, nor it's director, nor the star-cast, were known to the audience, the first response was very poor. But, day by day, word of mouth started making *Aulad* slowly popular with the public.

Ms Jaddan Bai (Nargis' mother) was a well-known Producer/Director in Bombay in those days. She was so charmed by the movie, she saw it several times with her family, her friends and with her film unit. Being an 'intellectual' artist herself she praised my penmanship. The critics hailed me as "the man who writes with tears, not ink."

As *Aulad* became increasingly popular, I used to go to the theatre each day to see the outcome of at least one show. Jaddan Bai was very keen to meet the Director of the movie, a Pandit Kidar Sharma. She had told the manager of the cinema, that since she came to see the movie every third day, she would like to meet Mr. Sharma whenever he showed up at the theatre. One day when she came to see the movie at 6:30 pm. for the sixth time, I also happened to be present. During the intermission I was ceremoniously taken to the manager's office, where Jaddan Bai was eagerly waiting for me.

The manager introduced me to Jaddan Bai saying, "This is Kidar Sharma from Bengal, the director of *Aulad*". Being an outspoken woman who used four letter words with regular frequency, and being a large woman with a heavy bosom and matching hips she remarked, "Allah, don't tell me this dubla-patla *laonda* (this skinny lad) has made this fine film." I sat beside her, and in my own style said "Madam, talent has nothing to do with weight, and brains and gray matter are not proportional to size. I am glad you like my movie. You have great taste."

Since Jaddan Bai also had a keen sense of humour she was pleased with my remark. Our conversation turned to other movie makers and she said. "Mr. Mehboob Khan made *Aurat* (woman) and Shri Shantaram made '*Aadmi*' (man)..." I interrupted her and said: "But it was Kidar Sharma who created '*Aulad*' (the progeny)." Jaddan Bai laughed and shook my hands, we had an instant liking for one another. Because she was very fond of poetry she loved my ghazals and my sharp sense of humour. I eventually directed her daughter Nargis in *Jogan* (the nun) in 1950.

When I returned to Calcutta Mr. R. Sharma told me that the movie had fared much better in the North. He also indicated that he had acquired the rights to Mr. Bhagwati Charan Verma's novel 'Chitralekha' and though initially, he wanted to produce and direct it himself, he now wanted me to write and direct it. I read the novel, and felt it resembled the French novel *Thais* written by Anatole France. It was a very powerful subject, but I felt that for cinema I would have to rewrite a number of the scenes, and adapt the novel. I told Mr. Sharma about my plans, and he agreed promising me his full support and cooperation. My only demand was that the title role of *Chitralekha* be played by Mehtab. Miss Mehtab was not a well known actress. She had worked in some B-grade stunt movies in Bombay. But I felt that she was perfect for the role. She arrived in Calcutta, and turned up in her own big Buick car. She wanted to impress me and pretended to act like royalty. She seemed to have bathed in some perfume because you could smell her aroma from a mile away. She also had a thing going for Mr. R. Sharma, and so I had to handle her with kid gloves. I chose Gyani to play the ascetic Kumar Giri and for the role of Bij Gupta, the lover, I selected a Maharashtrian actor Mr. B. Nandrekar. Since Romola was not keen to work in a costume movie, I selected a newcomer, a schoolteacher with a very innocent face, by the name of Miss Monica Desai, to play the role of Yashodra, despite her inexperience.

Before I could start the movie I received a letter from my father-in-law from Rawalpindi. My wife insisted we should go and visit them, as well as my parents in Narowal since both sets of parents were happy with my success. So I sent my wife, Prabha and Billy to my in-laws and I decided to take Vikram with me to Narowal first.

My youngest brother Kesho, a young lad of 18 was thrilled to see me. He was very proud of my accomplishments and had requested me earlier to get him a film projector, so that he could show his friend, clippings of movies at home. So I had bought a small home projector from Calcutta. It was a small hand crank projector that required a kerosene lamp, since there was no electricity in the village, and it had two loops to thread the film. I brought the projector and about two feet of film, but he wanted to run a longer film to show everyone. I told him that I also had another 200 feet of film that was just a test piece of Monica Desai. I gave it to him. He was delighted. Due to the long length of the film clip, the projector could overheat, I cautioned him, because films in those days were highly inflammable.

My sister Guro had also come home with her three daughters so it was a rare family re-union. That evening I decided to go to Rawalpindi with my son. Kesho escorted me to the railway station and insisted on carrying my small suitcase. I had a beautiful warm jacket which Kesho found irresistible and he at last said. "*Bhapaji* (elder brother), can you give me your jacket. I love it very much. You have given so many nice shirts to Himmat Bhaiya." But I was very mean and refused to part with the jacket. He just smiled and helped us get in the train and as the train moved, Kesho like all small children ran for some distance with the train waving wildly, which delighted my son who waved back till they could barely see each other. It was as if they were waving good bye for the last time.

January, 9th, 1940 was a day I will never forget. My son and I were the only two passengers in the compartment once we crossed the town of Jehlam. The temperature as we headed north turned to a freezing sub-zero and we were not accustomed to the cold weather. The train was still about fifty miles from our destination Rawalpindi when it stopped at a small station. Vikram's teeth were chattering, he had a fever and badly needed a hot cup of milk. I looked for a stall in vain. I got down to get some help and saw a small tea stall a few yards away, as I approached the stall, the train suddenly without any warning started moving. Vikram was all alone in the compartment and so I dashed after the train and grabbed it just in the nick of time. When I reached the compartment the terrified sick child was sitting there crying, and when I reached him he clung to me.

We reached my father-in-law's house the next morning and was shocked to see that my wife and the two younger children were preparing to go to the Railway Station, to catch the same train that departed in a couple of hours back to

Narowal. As I entered my wife handed me a telegram which read 'Kesho burnt seriously, come soon' We hurried back to the station and it was the most anguishing, and the longest journey back. When we reached our home at Narowal, I was told by my father that my dear, youngest brother had already died. My father took me to the roof and from a distance he pointed to a field where a pyre was still smoldering and he said, "You see that dark whiff of smoke, that is my son, my Kesho. Reaching the clouds...Reaching the heavens."

Kesho had been showing my film clip to my brother and sister and her three children. When suddenly the projector had overheated and the film caught fire. To save everyone from the inferno he wrapped his arms around the flaming projector. He was instantly engulfed in flames, and he received severe third degree burns. The children had also suffered slight burns and lay groaning in their beds. My mother who could not control her tears said "Kesho was entertaining the children with the film projector that you gave him, in that room. The projector caught fire and when we reached him he was seen holding the reel and screaming at everyone to run for their lives. Your father picked the earthen pitcher containing cold water and poured it on him to extinguish the burning boy, while I tried to help put out the flames with my hands. Your father tried to carry him, but he said he could walk to his bed."

I could see the blistered hands of my mother as she spoke. Then my father said. "He was in great agony but he would not show his pain, he only wanted me to send you a telegram immediately. I rushed out in search of a doctor, but in a place like Narowal it is impossible to get medical help at that time of the night." Then my mother added, "He asked for a glass of water and by the time I brought it to him he had closed his eyes for ever, leaving without quenching his thirst" as she sobbed bitterly.

I felt guilty and ashamed of myself. I had even refused to give him the jacket he wanted, and I felt responsible for having given him that dangerous toy, without having warned him sufficiently about the inflammable film and the kerosene lamp. I felt that this was another heavy price I was paying, on account of films. I had written, "*Bhagwan jo tera bhi bhagwan koye hoota, hum dakhate phir kiyun kur araam say tu soata*." (God, if there was another God above you, I'd like to see how well You could have rested.)

After this grim tragedy, I returned to Calcutta, but I could not start work. Finally Mr. R. Sharma consoled and advised me that the best thing was to start working to forget my sorrow. I also received a note from Mr. D.K. Bose which said "I must see you soon about an urgent matter."

That evening I went to Mr. Bose's house. He was most courteous and said "Kidar my boy, I want to discuss business. Tell me how much you received for directing *Aulad* and *Chitralekha*." I told him that I had been contracted to do two films for Rs. 20,000 and that one was released and I was ready to start *Chitralekha*." He looked at me and after thinking for a moment said, "I will pay you Rs. 15,000 if you write the dialogue and songs for my next movie Nartaki." I smiled because I remembered that this man was the same person who had refused to give me Rs. 5 more a month when I had begged him. So I asked him, "God! Do you think I deserve so much money?" "Yes, yes. Of course you do." He replied.

I told him that I had already signed with the Film Corporation of India and could not go back on my commitment. But he suggested that I continue making my new movie but also write the dialogue and songs for *Nartaki* and that way I would not be doing anything illegal. I then replied that I had a problem, because both *Chitralekha* and *Narkati* had identical themes, since they both dealt with the same subject matter of a dancer and a saint. And I could not be impartial enough. Saying, "Sorry, I am first a gentleman and then a writer." My refusal irritated Mr. Bose who shot back. "Look Kidar you don't stand a chance against me in this race. New Theaters and I, along with R.C. Boral and Leela Desai are giants and you are still a kid. Also the biggest stars, Sadhna Bose and Madhu Bose, are producing *Rajnartaki* on exactly the same subject. My film will be produced in English and Hindi, we will be spending lakhs of Rupees. You will be crushed, so be sensible and accept my offer." I simply rose and said, "Sorry, Perhaps we will meet again after our films are released."

I plunged myself in my work even more fervently. Before starting the shooting of *Chitralekha* I insisted that we rehearse and rehearse, the complete screen play. So the entire cast had to attend my training classes. Miss Mehtab had never liked rehearsals, so she resented the fact that she needed any rehearsing at all. Mr. R. Sharma my good friend persuaded her and told her to regard me as a teacher not a film director. He told her. "This movie will surely make someone a big star, and I want you to have all the luck." Being shrewd and smart Mehtab understood and started attending rehearsals regularly.

I chose my father's old friend from Punjab, Khan Sahib Jhanda Khan as my music director and since Mr. Gyani also had a good ear for music he approved of my choice. Khan Sahib Jhanda Khan was a short, bearded man who had composed some excellent music for the stage and had a thorough grasp of music. I then told him that I wanted the entire music to be composed in just one raga *Bhairvi*. He hesitated and said, " How many Rasgullas (sweets) can an audience enjoy? There should be some variety." I replied. "That depends on the person who makes the Rasgullas, and since you are a great master and chef, I am sure you will do a great job."

Khan Sahib was a highly religious man who prayed five times a day, as required by the Islamic religion. So he went inside to say his namaz (prayer) and upon emerging he said, "Sharmaji, I had a word with the Almighty and he has asked me to accept the challenge because He will be present at the harmonium when I compose the music. I shall therefore be able to produce at least 12 compositions which will all be in the same raga *Bhairvi*."

In this film, I had even bared a beauty on the silver screen for the first time with such finesse, in a bathing scene by Miss Mehtab, that nothing was revealed, but it created an illusion of great feminine charm. This scene created a controversy. Even the great writer Khwaja Ahmed Abbas praised the movie for its writing and its aesthetic charm.

Before we started shooting the bathing scene, I took my heroine Mehtab aside and explained to her how and why I was doing the scene. She said, "If the story demands this scene, I see no vulgarity in it, and so I am not afraid to strip, because we have no ugliness to hide. However I do have one condition. I consider my director to be just like my father and I will only strip if you ask everyone to clear the set. Since you are a good photographer yourself, please ask the cameraman to set the lights and the camera using a double, and when the set is cleared of everyone, you will be the only one with me and I will gladly perform. When you say the word action I will strip and enter the marble tub and enact the scene where I have to wash my body with a lotus flower till I hear the word 'cut'... but there should be no retakes." I agreed and Mehtab gracefully and beautifully performed the scene, which the critics raved about, and the audience loved.

Since the resources of Film Corporation of India were meagre we did have many difficulties. Mr. R. Sharma had arranged all the finances as well as he could and we had planned the film to the last detail. When I was in the throes of completing the last scene of the film, there were more difficulties, and someone had obtained a court order to lock up the studio. I needed just half an hour to complete the shot, so I asked my younger brother Himmat Rai to stall the official, and to take him out for a cup of tea or whatever he wanted to eat. This gave me just enough time to complete the shooting, and I knew that Mr. Bose had no such problems in his movies.

During the first trial of the movie none of the bosses were happy, in fact they seemed disappointed. They were disappointed from the start, when they heard the opening title music played by the great Shahnai player Bismillah Khan. At that time Bismillah Khan was a timid young man from Banaras. The bosses felt that the entire effort was a waste of film and so unceremoniously released the movie at the New Cinema in Calcutta. Now New Cinema belonged to our rivals, the New Theaters. The result was that it was an utter disaster. The staff of the cinema discouraged people from seeing the movie, advising them not to waste their hard earned money on such a lousy movie, and spreading rumours that the director was an amateur who had been rejected even as a third assistant to Mr. Bose. The film hardly ran for one week, it was a total flop.

To add insult to injury the author of the novel Shri B. C. Verma who ran a small Hindi newspaper for the big Sethias (merchants) wrote a stinging editorial chastising the director of the movie, and accusing me of ruining his work of art. I was even ridiculed by the New Theaters staff. I felt totally humiliated and defeated. The Film Corporation Studio was already sealed by a court order, and the entire unit of the movie *Chitralekha* was now jobless. Only one person was persistently hopeful. Mr. R. Sharma never lost faith. Destiny is an author with a great sense of suspense and when Mr. R. Sharma released the movie in the North it just took off. It became an overnight hit. People called it a masterpiece. And surprisingly, if anyone created the slightest disturbance, even during the title score, the audience threw the person out. They were so enraptured.

Khan Sahib had accomplished what seemed impossible when he composed the most beautiful music, all in one raga. His rare compositions gave the film a big boost when it was finally properly released. *Chitralekha* became known for its music, its performances, its philosophical depth, the writing and for its sheer beauty. It became a masterpiece We had all profited, Mehtab and Gyani were now big names. I was hailed as a great director, writer, and philosopher. We had even outclassed Mr. Bose and his large contingent. *Chitralekha* brought me immense honor, and fame. I was now considered a great writer and a skillful director. But in spite of all the praise and the adulation I was still unemployed. So I wrote to Prithviraj, who had moved to Bombay, to help and see if there was any opportunity of a job in Bombay.

Khan Sahib was immensely acclaimed for his music for songs like *Saiyan sanvare bhaye banvare, haan neel kummal muskaye, punchi ritu aaye ritu jaaye, naiya dheeray dheeray jaana, tum javo javo bhagwan bane*. In that last song, the singer tells God ; *Tum unkey jo tum ko dhayaane jo naam rutten mukti paiyan, hum paap karen aur door hutten tum paar karo to jaane*. The same thought is expressed in Omar Khayyam's little known translation by Whinfield:

'If Grace be Grace, and Allah gracious be,
Adam from paradise, why banished He?
Grace to poor sinners shown, is Grace indeed,
In Grace hard earned by work, no Grace I see.

Chapter 12

"The only true happiness comes from squandering ourselves for a purpose."

John Mason Brown

Prithviraj wrote back and asked me to reach Bombay at once, so that he could arrange an interview with Seth Chandulal Shah, who had seen my movie and liked what I had done. I travelled to Bombay, but left my family behind in Calcutta. When I arrived in Bombay, the first thing I did was to call on my friend Prithviraj. He was delighted to hear my voice after such a long time and said, "I know that you have come in search of work, but let me give you one piece of advice — Do not negotiate with anyone till you have met Mr. Chandulal Shah, who is very keen to hire you for Ranjit Movietone. He has seen *Chitralekha* several times at the Opera House, the cinema hall which belongs to him. I will telephone you tomorrow, after fixing your appointment with Mr. Shah." Next day I was told: "Meet Mr. Shah at 1.00 p.m. sharp, please be punctual as Mr. Shah's time is very precious." I reached Ranjit Studios at 12.30 and found Prithviraj waiting for me. He embraced me and asked me to sit comfortably in the verandah, as he had to run and complete a shot for the film he was working in. This was the famous verandah, (in which I waited), where the renowned Seth C.J. Shah used to sit along with Madam Gouharbai, his partner, and hold Darbar (court) like Akbar the Great, and discuss stories, scenes and songs with his *Rattans* (Jewels) as he called them.

Exactly at 1p.m., Mr. Shah arrived in his big car, and after making some urgent telephone calls, looked at his watch and asked his peon Rukma to fetch Mr. Prithviraj. As soon as Prithviraj arrived Mr. Shah demanded, "It is going to be 10 past 1 .p.m., where is your friend Mr. Kidar Sharma?" Prithvi smiled and pointing to the sofa said, "Right in front of you, and he is keen to talk to you when you have the time." Mr. Shah adjusted his glasses, looked at me from head to foot, while I greeted him with folded hands and a big smile, a most important gesture when you badly need a job — and I needed one badly. Mr. Shah was puzzled and inquired. "Is this the genius who is responsible for creating a masterpiece like *Chitralekha*? This youngster is so ordinary looking, so thin..." "And very humble", I added, "Yes, I am Pundit Kidar Sharma the ugly duckling, but you are not hiring me for my face. You will need me, if at all to stand behind the camera as your film director and writer. Appearances are deceptive; beauty does not always possess brains, to prove my point all you have to do is look in the mirror."

While Prithviraj was not happy with my frank response, Gouharbai who was Mr. Chandulal's constant companion said, "Yes Mr. Shah is also dark but look at his achievements."

Mr. Chandulal Shah then said. "Well it is decided Mr. Sharma you are joining and I will start you on a salary of Rs. 3000 per month starting from today."

I thanked him and responded. "Sir you are silver headed but golden hearted."

I never expected Mr. Shah to be so benevolent because Rs. 3000 per month was a very good salary. I then told him. "Sethji I am extremely grateful for your most generous offer, but first I have to return to Calcutta and fetch my family, so perhaps we could start my salary from the day I report for work at Ranjit Studio." Then he asked me to meet him in the evening at the Opera House before he left.

I met Mr. Shah at 5 pm. at the Opera House and he handed me Rs. 5000 saying. "Here is some money to bring your family from Calcutta comfortably. Rs 2500 will be adjusted against your salary when you begin work, but Rs 2500 is a gift from Gouharbai who enjoyed chatting with you." I took the money and thanked him, then I inquired if I needed to sign any receipt for the payment. He retorted back. "We know whom to trust." I left for Prithviraj's house and thanked him for the favour. He told me to thank Lord Ganpati since Ganpati Day was being celebrated that day, and in Bombay it is a major festival. He also added that I had suffered enough to achieve my goal in films, and this was my just reward.

Madam Gouharbai had a keen and ready wit. She once said, "Kidar, you have Tarzan eyes that jump from limb to limb."

I joined Ranjit Studios on the 3rd. of October 1941. I brought back my family and my favourite green car from Calcutta. I narrated two story ideas to Mr. Shah for his approval. He selected the off-beat subject 'Armaan' for my first film for Ranjit Studios. It was the story of an angry young prince who goes to college, and becomes an atheist. He believes in the miracle of science rather than in the Almighty. One day in an accident in the laboratory, he loses his vision. He meets with a beautiful village girl who befriends and helps him, and she being the opposite – a true believer in God, asks the Lord to pardon him.

The opening song of the film Baitho meri ankhon may tumhe duniya dikhayun (Come, let me show you the world through the eyes of love) was praised by both Mr. Shah and Miss Gouharbai. When we came to selecting the stars for the movie I insisted that we hire Mr. Motilal, as my Hero and Shamim as my Heroine. Shamim, was the niece of the top star Khurshid, of Ranjit Movietone. Mr. Shah said, "If you take Shamim, Khurshid will never work with you in any film, as she is very jealous of her young and charming niece Shamim, and as for taking Motilal, I have an understanding with him, that he will choose his director. Therefore you have to meet Motilal and get his confirmation."

I have always been a great admirer of Motilal, who was a natural and a powerful actor. Motilal had never seen my *Aulad* or my *Chitralekha*. In his opinion, I was some Bengali Babu, some pseudo-intellectual, who thought he was a genius. So when I met him in his make-up room next morning, he was quite arrogant, and said, "Bengali Babu..." I interrupted him saying "I am not a Bengali Babu, I am a Punjabi..."

He interjected. "I have three conditions, you say yes to all my conditions, and I shall say yes to your proposal."

So I asked him to let me know his three conditions and he said, "First I shall not work on Sunday as I have a date with race horses, the second condition is that, as I punctually report for work at 9 am I shall walk away at 6 pm, not bothering whether that shot is o.k. or needs another retake, and the third condition is I do not rehearse, and I am told you are very fond of rehearsals."

I smiled and said. "I agree to all these three conditions." He said. "Then I shall work in 'Armaan'." My assistant from Calcutta, Rajinder Sharma was with me, he asked me why I had become so spineless in Bombay when in Calcutta I dictated. "You were the great director once", he said. I exclaimed. "Just wait and watch, there is time yet to put things in better perspective !"

It was Saturday, and I told Motilal, we had only one shot to do for the day, if it finished in twenty minutes the entire unit would thank him for the early pack-up. In Ranjit Studios this was unheard of. He smiled and said "Yes Sharmaji, I fully agree with you." I responded. "I am very self exacting, I want to make sure that you capture the essence of the shot, in which the blind hero tumbles and painfully requests the heroine to lend a helping hand." Motilal retorted "So you can act too! Show me how it is to be done." I replied. "No, I just try to mimic great stars like you, and pick up subtle pointers whenever I can." I performed the tragic scene and

Motilal watched attentively. Then we set up the lights and the camera position ready to shoot. Motilal the great did the shot, but added some more lines to make the shot more absorbing — everyone applauded and I said, "O. K. that's fine, we can all go home." But Motilal had some hesitation and said, "No, No, wait I would like to do the shot again, I think I missed something and am not quite pleased." I merely said. "It's fine if you want to try it again." Again Motilal did his best, and again he knew that he had failed to fully capture what I had shown him earlier. He was becoming increasingly frustrated with himself, and kept repeating the take. I approved every one of his takes but he insisted, and demanded that he be given one more opportunity. I was so confident of his pride in his own professionalism, that I knew he would not accept anything merely satisfactory as good work.

It was now edging close to 9:00 pm. and Motilal was still struggling with the scene, trying to perfect his performance and timing. He had forgotten the rule that he had laid down at the onset. He was on the verge of tears and said. "How can I achieve what you captured when you showed me how to portray this scene."

I replied. "As they say — practice makes perfect. I am a firm believer in rehearsals, and rehearsals are a Sadhna, a dedicated practice alone which gives us achievement."

He hugged me and we became the best of friends from that day onwards. He also wanted to be present for those scenes where he was not required, saying that he wanted to assist me in the film. He even took the trouble to come and feed everyone with a big basket of home made samosas which his loving mother had made. As a friend, he once told me that his mother was very upset because she said, "Ever so often a woman telephones, and when I ask who it is, she replies it is Kidar Sharma." Since I do have an effeminate high pitched voice, he could now crack a joke at my expense and he added, "Voices too can be deceptive." Motilal was one of the most natural and effortless actors, he was fluid, I made other films with him subsequently. He was unbelievably good at making everyone comfortable, to get the best out of them, with his charm. "*Charm: that quality in others of making us more satisfied with ourselves*." – Henry F. Amiel.

Dada Gogte was the Ace Cameraman at Ranjit Studios, and Mr. Ambre was merely his assistant. Ambre had hoped to get a chance to become a cameraman, and he approached and begged me to give him an opportunity. In those days Ranjit Studios mass produced films, like a factory, with dozens in the making on some days. I agreed to give Ambre a chance, and took full responsibility for the consequences. I have always encouraged and fostered new and young talent. It is one thing that I am very proud of and feel I have done a good deed in this 'dog eat dog' world of entertainment. When Mr. Shah saw what Ambre had produced, he praised and thanked me for training his staff too. I made many films for Ranjit. Some were good, some bad and some to which I was indifferent. And then one day out of the blue I decided that I would stop mass producing films and become a producer. But more about this later.

One of the films I was making for Ranjit was *Vishkanya* starring Prithviraj, Sadhna Bose and Surinder Nath. During the shooting I felt that my friend Prithviraj seemed sad and dejected although he never said so. I finally could stand it no longer and taking him aside asked, "If it is not personal, and if you can share your problem with me, and take me into your confidence, I would like to help in any way that I can, because something seems to be bothering you."

He replied. "Kidar I am worried about my son Raju. Adolescence is making him go astray. I sent him to college but his mind is on girls..." I thought for a while and said, "Put him under my tutelage, I am like a teacher. I will teach the boy my art and perhaps some lessons. I may be harsh but I am not a tyrant. But you must not interfere and let me bring the boy up in a *Guru-Chela* (Teacher-pupil) relationship. I will make him my assistant director."

The next day Raju (Raj Kapoor) came to Ranjit with his father, and as is customary with the upbringing of the Kapoor clan, he bent down and touched my feet. I smiled and reminded him of the time when he was just a little boy in Calcutta, and had asked me holding up a strip of film: "Uncle why do the pictures in these frames move?" and I had replied: "Son, when I do find out one day, I will teach you the secret, well the time has come and I would like you to learn something from me now." I made him my third assistant and his job was to be the clapper boy. I wanted him to start from the lowest rung. Raju was always naughty but I must admit, my favourite. Every time we were ready to shoot I would instruct Raju to bang the clap. He always replied enthusiastically and loudly, "Yes Uncle." But before doing so, he would comb his hair and frame his face to the camera, as if he was posing, beaming a smile to the camera, and announce the shot before the clap stick. I watched this little enactment day after day, but I ignored it as another childish prank.

Once we had gone on an outdoor shoot to a place called Ghodbundar. It was a beautiful spot and we waited several hours for a shot where the main character was to do a single take, because it was a 'sunset' scene. The actor was playing a bearded king, and so had a false beard on. We wanted to shoot a symbolic shot depicting the king's downfall with the sun setting in the background. We framed the shot, waiting for the sun to be in just the right position before we commenced shooting. I instructed and begged Raju not to comb his hair or take too much time with the clap because the sun was setting fast and I had only one chance to shoot the scene, I shouted. "Raj, are you ready?" "Yes, Uncle!" he replied. I shouted, "Camera" which was a cue for Raj to start the clap, but once again he first combed his hair and framed his face in the camera with his usual smile, and totally oblivious of where the clap was, he banged the clapper board. The actors beard was caught in the clapper board, and as Raj moved away from the camera, he yanked the beard completely off the actor. The actor playing the king was dumb-struck and just stood there, as the sun slowly set and moved out of frame. I was livid, we had waited for hours and had traveled more than 40 miles to take this shot. I could not control my temper, and in total rage and fury I called Raj. He approached me with a faint smile and when he came to me, I slapped his face hard in front of the entire unit, and a large group of spectators, who always collect when one is shooting in India.

I thought Raj would snap back with something like, "You don't pay me enough so I do not deserve this abuse," or "I am the son of a big star, how dare you strike me!" But the boy just silently slunk away and smiled back. I had hit him so hard that my fingers had left an impression on his face. I announced to the staff to pack up and said that we would come here again on the next day to finish the shot. There was complete silence as everybody quietly packed and left.

That night I could not sleep. I was ashamed of what I had done, but now I understand the reason why Raj combed his hair and always smiled at the camera. It was because the boy was most keen to face the camera, and not stand behind it.

The following day, when we returned to the studio after completing the sunset shot, I called Raj and asked him to see me in my office. He walked in timidly and in his usual jovial manner asked, "Do I have to offer the other cheek?" "No." I replied, "But I have come to an important decision." And I handed him a contract. A contract of Rs. 25,000 to be the Hero in my next film. A film that I wanted to produce myself. He was stunned and amazed and began apologizing saying. "No, Uncle! Don't ruin yourself for my sake. I am just a joker. I am a bit too plump to be a star. I am a novice. I am not good enough. Please hire someone else. Really I am unworthy..." I stopped him and said, "Son, you did not cry when I hit you yesterday, but today you are nearly in tears." To which he retorted "Sir I can digest aggression specially if

I am at fault, but kindness always brings tears to my eyes and chokes my heart. Thank you for your kindness and your trust."

We were silent for some time, and then he finally admitted, "Yes, I would love to face the camera and show you my acting talent. I will obey you and not let you down." I hugged the boy and he whispered, "Please Uncle, please hire the little girl Mumtaz as your heroine, I like her and I am sure you also admire her innocent and angelic face, besides she is a bit shorter than me."

Although Mumtaz was still a teenager and also totally inexperienced, I hired her to play the female lead. Her father Attaulla, who was a shrewd man, was extremely grateful. But I had not yet discussed my decision or my choices of stars with Miss Gouharbai and Mr. Chandulal Shah, nor my plan to become a producer.

So the next day when Mr. Shah and Miss Gouharbai were alone, I told Mr. Shah, "Sethji, I would like to produce a picture called 'Bechara Bhagwan' (Poor God). But I promise that I will work from morning till 9. pm. for Ranjit Studios, and then I will go and shoot my own movie for 3 hours each day. I assure you that there will be no problems for Ranjit Studios, since I still need the money, not having adequate money for my own picture."

Miss Gouharbai remarked. "I like the title of your movie." But Mr. Shah was silent for a long, long time and then asked "How much cash do you have to start your movie?" I responded. "I have Rs.1,00,000 (one lakh) in the State Bank of India." Mr. Shah shot back, "I will give you a cheque of one lakh Rupees, that way you will have two lakhs to start your movie and I will become a partner. I am sure you will not mind that, and will accept my proposal." "Sir, I am grateful and honoured." I remarked. And Mr. Shah said, "Go ahead now. You will be a producer as well as a director Mr. Kidar Sharma."

I was very happy and wanted to help some deserving people, by giving them a chance in this venture. The first name was Vasudev Bhatkar, who had once come to me for music notation of songs of *Chitralekha* for H.M.V. as he worked for them. I sent word to Bhatkar to meet me on Sunday at 10 a.m. sharp. So on Sunday Bhatkar arrived punctually, and greeting me at the studio gate meekly said, "Yes, Sharmaji, I am at your service."

I told him. "Do you remember, some time back when you used to come to my house for notations of Jhande Khan's music of *Chitralekha* you had said 'I want to be a music director too — I do not wish to work all my life, as a Harmonium player at H. M. V., where I am employed. But then who will take the risk of engaging me as a music director?" He said with his head bent low. "Yes I remember." I told him, "I too have not forgotten it Mr. Bhatkar!" Then I took out five Thousand Rupee notes, quite an amount in those days, and offering them to Bhatkar saying, "Here, this is the amount, for my music director for my film *Bechara Bhagwan*, which I am going to produce in partnership which Mr. Chandulal Shah." "Why are you paying me the full amount of my remuneration in advance Sharmaji – this five thousand hard cash – I have never seen a Thousand Rupee note till today. Thanks a lot." "No Mr. Bhatkar, this is only the signing amount, you will get a total of Rs. 25000, for your entire work." I told him. Bhatkar only repeated "Twenty Five Thousand! " in stunned surprise.

On Monday when Mr. Shah called me to enquire about the progress of the film, I told him, "The music director is finalized." He asked. "Who?, I told him. "Mr. Bhatkar, a genius." Miss Gauhar said with amazement. "Never heard of this genius." Mr. Shah removing his glasses and staring at me, asked, "What about the cast of Bechara Bhagwan?" So I told him. "Sethji my hero is Raju, Prithvi's son." Sethji asked about the Heroine and my reply was "Mumtaz". Baby Mumtaz had not yet become known as Madhubala. He suddenly got up and said. "I am in a hurry. Tomorrow when we meet we shall talk more about this subject. You know that as your partner in this venture, I have the right to ratify all decisions."

Next day I met Mr. Shah, but he was under the impression that, when I said Mumtaz, I had meant Mumtaz Shanti the famous star of Ranjit in those days and not Baby Mumtaz. When he spoke of Mumtaz Shanti, I tried to correct the misunderstanding by saying that Mumtaz Shanti would look like Raj's mother, therefore Baby Mumtaz was the correct choice and my choice also.

He was so shocked to hear this from me that an awkward situation arose between us, Mr. Shah's demand was, "I want my money back, my One Lakh rupees back, I shall not risk my money on this movie, unless you throw Baby Mumtaz, Bhatkar and Raj Kapoor out, and replace them with saleable names. If you do not agree, then my decision is that you must return my money!" Everyone was ridiculing me for my folly. But I had already started the shooting of my film, which was now renamed *Neel Kamal*. In those days all the workers and artists were paid monthly salaries, and commitments had already been made. The contract system or per day system was yet to come into vogue.

I always paid my staff by the 10th of every month. It so happened I could not, now pay anyone his monthly dues. I was sitting, sad and pensive, in my room at Ranjit Studios, when one of my favourite artist Nazirabai quietly entered my room. She was a Hindu girl, in her youth she had married a Muslim boy who loved her, and had changed her name from Nishi to Nazirabai. She was holding a packet wrapped in a blue handkerchief with white polka dots, and she was smiling at me. Before she could utter a word I angrily snapped, "I am not dead as yet Nazirabai, just give me a little more time and I shall pay you your salary... so please leave me alone at this moment." Poor Nazirabai moved away without saying a word but left the bundle she was carrying. I first thought that she knows how I love to eat, so she must have brought me some food wrapped in the handkerchief.

I opened the bundle and was amazed to find Rs.17,000 and some gold ornaments. The poor lady had out of respect and regard brought me this money to help me continue the shooting of my film *Neel Kamal*. I was very touched by this gesture and equally ashamed of the way I had angrily shouted at her. She had come merely to help me out. I ran after her and caught up with her. She was sobbing when I reached her on the staircase. Her eyes were red and she stood trembling with emotion. I was humbled and with folded hands I begged and implored her to forgive me. I thanked her for her kind gesture but insisted that she take her money and her ornaments back and, if she wished, she could bring me some *bajhia* (snacks) the next day. I told her that in the next few days I would be able to secure a loan to ease her fears about my financial turmoil. She reluctantly obeyed and left.

I once again was put in a position where I had to send an S.O.S. to *Bhagwan* (God) via my grandmother's favorite *Bhajan*. Soon I heard from Amravati about a territory (films are sold in India by territories) known as C.P.C.I. representing central India, in the film trade. I got an offer to sell the rights of my movie *Neel Kamal* to a distributor from there. They even agreed to my condition that I must receive rupees one lakh for signing. Such a demand had been unheard of in the industry in those days. The distributor simply said on the phone, "Yes, Sharmaji, we will do as you say. I will personally bring the cash tomorrow." The next day he came and bought off two more territories of my movie. Soon, except for Bengal, all the territories were sold off even before the film was completed. And the movie did not have any well known stars in it, except Begum Para. Everyone was surprised including Mr. Taimur and Miss Begum Para, who praised me for my courage, and for my will to stand up against all odds.

On completion of the movie I requested Mr. Shah and Miss Gouharbai, who I always considered to be an angel, to honour me by coming, and viewing the first trial of the movie. They saw the first rough cut of the movie and were greatly impressed. Then Mr. Shah said that if there was any territory outstanding he would like to buy it at a price that I could dictate, and was prepared to pay Rs. 10,000 just for signing. I replied. "Sir you are very noble and kind, please take the territory that I have left, Bengal and adjust it against the Studio bills that I owe Ranjit Studios."

I had completed the movie but I needed another Rs. 60,000 badly. I approached Gouharbai and asked her, "What should I do?" She said, "Look Kidar, Sethji has a very high regard for your work and your character. Tell him you need a loan and he will say – Yes." So when I approached him he did exactly as she had predicted. He handed me a sealed envelope and after leaving his office

I opened it to find that the envelope contained not Rs.60,000 that I had asked for, but Rs. 100,000. I thought that he had loaned me an additional forty thousand so that I would not have to approach him again for financial help. But he had left a little note inside which read '*Neel Kamal* has been very profitable. We want you to share some of the profits with us'. It was signed by Chandulal, Chotubhai, and Ratibai, Mr. Chandulal's two cousins.

Neel Kamal brought me luck, and gave Raj Kapoor his first break in films as an actor. I had told him that I had carried him as a child, and he was welcome to use my shoulders. Raj reminded me of Issac Newton 'If I have seen further, it is by standing on the shoulders of giants'. It also made Mumtaz (later Madhubala), a recognized star and helped establish a name for my music director Bhatkar, who had changed his name to Snehal Bhatkar. The Snehal half was adopted from his daughter's name, because he was still working for H.M.V and did not want any legal hassles. He did a beautiful job by setting to music the song*Aankh jo dekhay hai dhooka khaye hai, dil jo aandha hai woh raha butlaiye hai*. Years later I wrote another piece that Madhubala fell so much in love with that she wanted it dedicated to her exclusively, like her private property, therefore this piece has never been used in any film: *Radha ko naa tursaa, shyam puchtayega, nain challak aaye toe brij beh jaayega*. (Radha admonishes Lord Krishna not to tease her lest the torrential deluge of her tears washes away Brij.)

I continued directing films for Ranjit Studios, and in 1943 hr I wrote a story called *Gouri*. It was a story set in Calcutta, woven around Durga Puja, a religious festival very popular in Bengal. It was a touching human story and highly emotional. When I narrated the story to Mr. Chandulal Shah and Miss Gouharbai they could not control their emotions and wept openly. Then Mr. Shah said, "Being a subject that is most familiar to Bengalis, I am afraid it might not be as meaningful to the rest of the masses in India, who do not appreciate the significance of Durga Puja. However, I would still like to make the movie, and I am prepared to send the unit to Calcutta to shoot the movie during this religious festival." I was thrilled with the story and anxious to start work. I insisted that the main role of *Khumar* — the effigy maker of the Goddess Durga, should be played by my old friend Prithviraj. Gouharbai then inquired. "But who will you cast as Gouri, the female lead?"

I replied that I could think of no one from our current set of stars that the Studio had signed up. I needed some one who was fresh and innocent, because the script demanded that, to do full justice to the plot. So I asked for some time to think about it and perhaps I would have a name by the next day. This subject was actually my gift to Miss Monica Desai, the younger sister of the star Leela Desai. Monica Desai was a schoolteacher who had the freshness and the innocence hard to find in big stars. She had played a small role in my film *Chitralekha* and had given quite a good performance. Years ago when we were working together I had promised her that when I got established, and when I have the right script, I would make her my main lead. She then said, "Sharmaji, they say you keep your word. I will keep my fingers crossed till that day."

The next day I told my bosses of my decision to hire Monica Desai. Mr. Shah agreed but inquired, "Would she move from Calcutta to Bombay where the bulk of the shooting will be done?" I told him that since this was a role of a lifetime for a struggling artist, any one would jump at the chance and agree to our terms and conditions. The big hearted Mr. Shah quietly took out Rs 5000 from his pocket and said, "Send her this amount as travelling money, and she will receive the rest when we sign a formal contract." When I spoke to Prithviraj about the choice, he was delighted and agreed wholeheartedly.

I sent Miss Desai the money and explained on the telephone that she should travel by first class and when she reaches Dadar Station in Bombay, she should get off and go to the first class ladies waiting room with her bag and baggage, and leave it there with an attendant. She could then freshen up, take a bath there, and then put on her best silk sari to make herself presentable. She should take a taxi to Ranjit Studio which was 5 minutes away and reach the studio by 2:30 p.m. I would then present her to Mr. Chandulal Shah and Miss Gouharbai. I then asked her if she had understood my instructions. And she replied that she had.

We waited anxiously for Miss Monica Desai's arrival that afternoon. Mr. Shah saw from his verandah that a woman was having an argument with the watchman. He inquired about the confusion and the watchman said, "Sir, a crazy woman thinks our Studio is a *dharamsala* (lodging house) and wants to enter with a smelly boy who is carrying her luggage." The magnanimous Mr. Shah told him to find out where she had come from, and who she wanted to meet? The man returned shortly saying "Sir, she is from Calcutta, a relative of Mr. Kidar Sharma." The kindhearted boss, told him to inform me to look after the lady, since he thought that she was a stranger to Bombay and my relative also. Little did Mr. Shah realize that this most ordinary looking, foolish woman was none other than Monica Desai, the star of his movie *Gouri*.

I was called from Studio No. 2, where I was shooting and was shocked to find Monica with bag and baggage. On learning her identity, Mr. Shah ordered me to arrange boarding and lodging for my heroine from Bengal. Then he got up, and along with Gouharbai drove away without saying a word. He was obviously annoyed but suppressed his rage, and my buddy Prithviraj felt very humiliated by Monica's foolishness. Monica the miser, just to save twelve annas, had put me in a very awkward situation.

Anyway I took her in my car, to the vacant apartment of a friend, and rented it for Rs. 60 per month. Then I took Monica to a restaurant for lunch. She felt I was sad and hurt and so she put her hand on mine and said, "When you help undeserving people, this is what happens." I was silent and she added, "Why has God made me so foolish, and my sister Leela so smart." She was now tearful and asked. "Can you pardon me Sharmaji?" I said, "Give me time" and I told her to rest for a day or two before I would take her back to the Studio.

Next day when Mr. Shah and Gouharbai came to the studio, he sent for me and taking me aside to Miss Gauharbai's room for privacy, he told me, "Look, I shall not go back on my word to produce *Gauri*, but I do not need to be part of any discussion, nor do I want to attend the shooting, the song recording sessions, or to see the rushes any more. When you have completed the movie and it is ready to be shown to the censor board I will view the film. Because enough is enough. I feel there is more to this than just finding a new face, and with a deep sigh, he stood up. I went back to the set to resume shooting, because in a few days we were to go to Calcutta to film the Durga Puja festival, which was fast approaching.

On the last set, a most interesting thing happened. The lady who was playing Prithviraj's domineering mother was a stage actress. When I asked her to rehearse the shot, prior to actual shooting, she was quite rude and said, "Son, I have

Kaka Kura also featured a black stallion as it's star. I think I actually saved his life since he could no longer race.

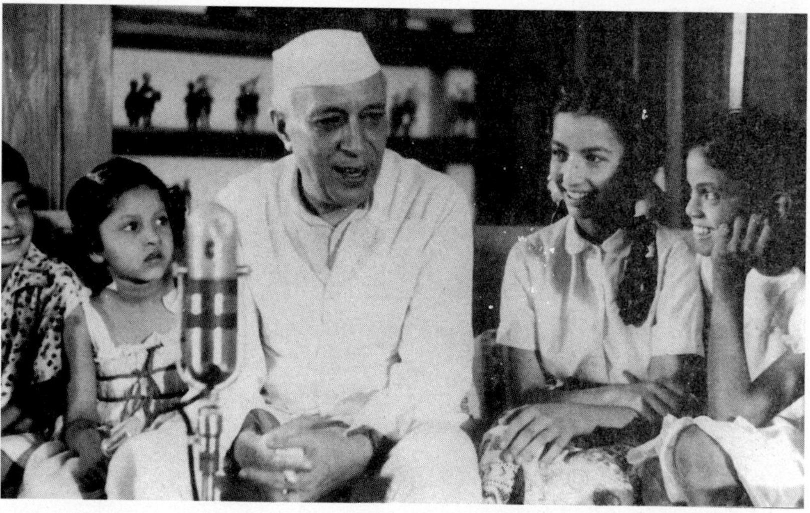

I even directed Pandit Nehru in a short Children's Film called *Bachhon Se Baathen.* The movie also included his grandsons. His daughter Indra Gandhi was the Vice-President of the Society at that time.

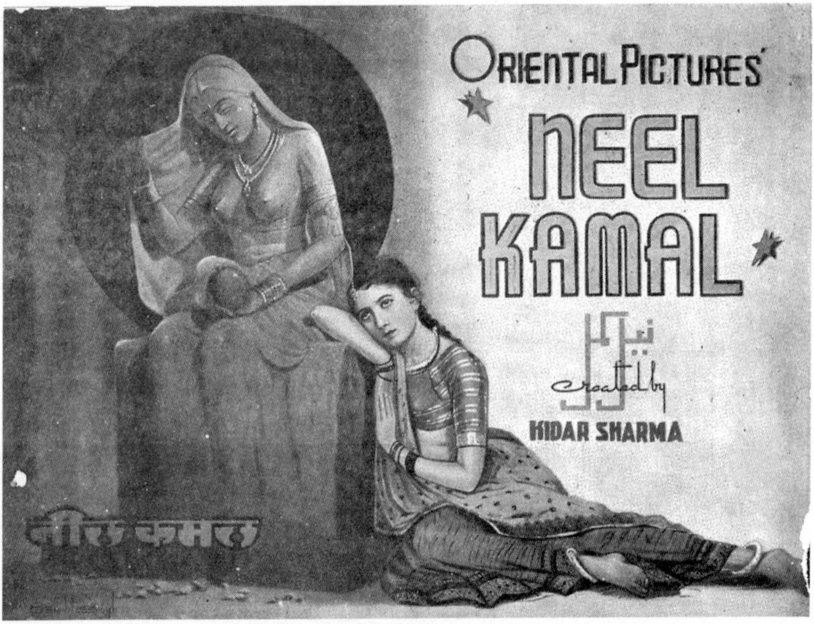

My sense of pride and my convictions have always forced my hand to gamble with my own fate rather than to bow to the whims of others. *Neel Kamal* was such a gamble It was the birth of not only my first independent venture as a Producer Director, but I also cultivated and introduced two of the greatest discoveries to Indian Films. Raj Kapoor and Madhubala. I was ridiculed for casting these unknowns in my movie. Both went on to became the most famous stars.

Geeta Bali in her first movie *Sohag Raat.* She gave a stunning performance as the woman who looses in love opposite such veterans as Begum Para and Bharat Bhushan. She was no older than a teenager in the film.

I even dared to play the main lead in my movie called *Neki aur Badi.* It co-starred both Geeta Bali and Madhubala. Madhubala, was one of the most beautiful Indian actress. In an interview at the height of her carrier, she said: "Kidar Sharma always does what he makes up his mind to do. He is the only man in our money-grabbing industry who never comprised his art for the sake of wealth or importance.... He is my guru and I am proud to be his disciple."

Begum Para was the only big star in *Neel Kamal*, both my main actors Raj Kapoor and Madhubala were newcomers and completely unknown.

I cast Geeta Bali and Raj Kapoor in *Bawre Nain.* Both had an excellent sense of rhythm. Raj always showed great respect for me, even when he was the biggest star. He would throw away his cigarette if I entered and always rushed to meet me, bowing down to touch my feet no matter who else was around. He has always considered me to be his Guru.

▶

Geeta Bali in *Bawre Nain* (top)
with Raj sitting near my feet. (below)

BAWRE
NAIN

The remake of *Chitralekha* had the biggest stars of that time.Meena Kumari, Ashok Kumar, Predeep Kumar and Mehmood. The music was composed by Roshan, yet in spite of this talented team, in my openion it did not match the earlier version that I had made.
Below:
With Meena Kumari while shooting.

In 1950 I made the movie *Jogan* for Ranjit Studio. It starred Nargis and Dilip Kumar. It was never revealed who the original writer was. It was none other than Chandulal Shah. It was his dream to produce this movie and he gave me the special honour of directing it, in spite of all the directors he had on his staff.
Nargis felt that despite her many other outstanding films like *Mother India* etc., her best film was *Jogan*.

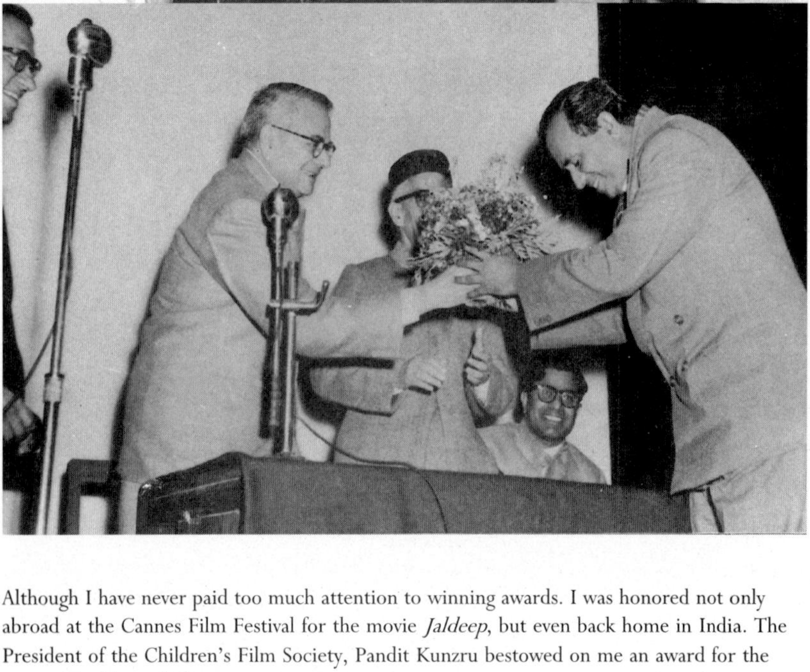

Although I have never paid too much attention to winning awards. I was honored not only abroad at the Cannes Film Festival for the movie *Jaldeep*, but even back home in India. The President of the Children's Film Society, Pandit Kunzru bestowed on me an award for the movie. I had brought honor to my country.

worked with giants like Agha Hashar when you were still a *dood pita bachha* (a milk drinking baby). Let us not waste time on rehearsals, start shooting and it will be fine." I was silent for a while and then said, "Madam I must do my duty, so I will demonstrate what I require by doing the scene once and then you can improve upon it." And then I sat down on a chair, which I have never done on the sets in my lifetime.

Being a shrewd lady she said, "Can we break for lunch now and resume in about an hour?" Since there was no fixed time when we broke for lunch at Ranjit Studio, I consented. When I reached my own room, there was a knock on the door and the peon said that the lady wanted me to go and meet her in her make-up room. I went to inquire what she needed.

The moment I entered her make-up room, she locked the room behind her and with open arms she said, "Son, embrace my, I am so proud of you. You really know your job well. But now sit down and listen to me." Just then there was a knock on the door and she went to it and returned with two cups of tea. She offered me one cup and said, "Son, today is the second time in my life that I have embraced a man. Being poor, my parents could not afford to get me married. My father was a cripple and my mother knew some people who knew Mr. Agha Hashar Kashmiri, the great stage actor. My mother requested that I be given some work on stage to make some money, which would be an enormous help. So that evening I put on my best sari and was taken to Mr. Agha for an interview. I was nervous and was trembling. I knew that I was no beauty, but I also knew that I was not bad looking either and, being a village girl, I was quite well built. Agha Hashar gave me some lines to recite. But they were in chaste Urdu, and since I am not that familiar with that language I had some trouble with the pronunciation of some of the words. However, I was still selected and taken to Calcutta to work with in Mr. Agha Hasar's plays on stage. I missed my parents and my friends at first but gradually I got so absorbed with my work that nothing mattered to me more than acting. One day during lunch break I was called to Mr. Agha's room. I went there, and just like I bolted the door after you came in, Mr. Agha did the same thing and to my surprise he said, "I am dying to embrace you." I replied, "Me too!" which brought a smile to his face and before he could come to me I continued, "You remind me of my elder brother, who had died of an accident. Hold me close to your heart, and permit me to tie a *Rakhi* on your wrist annually." Mr. Agha Hashar was dumfounded, but composed himself and graciously bent down and touched my feet and said, "You are like a Durga in my eyes. Please forgive me for having let an ugly thought cross my mind, but I am only human." Then she turned to me and said, "I hope you are not ashamed of me my son."

At last we completed the movie *Gouri* and the rough cut was ready for viewing. I approached Mr. Shah and invited him to review the movie. Mr. Shah was only accompanied by Miss Gouharbai to see this trial. Usually all the directors working for Ranjit would review a film at this stage. Now if Mr. Shah liked the movie or a particular scene he would rave about it in his native tongue Gujrati, but if he disliked the movie or a scene he would start abusing in Hindi and sometimes threw his *chappal* (sandal) at the screen. That was the trademark of the great Mr. Chandulal Shah.

The two of them sat in the front row and I sat behind them with my fingers crossed. In the movie there were some electrifying scenes between the two main characters, which were highly charged and very emotional. But there was no reaction from either Mr. Shah or Miss Gouharbai. They were both very silent and I too was silent waiting for a reaction. The movie came to an end, and after a few moments Mr. Shah rose followed by Miss Gouharbai. They quietly walked out and went down the stairs without a word to me. As I followed out of the projection room the operator came to me and silently whispered, "Sharmaji, your days in Ranjit Studios are numbered. I am sure you will be asked to collect your final cheque and will be leaving at 8:00 for the last time, unceremoniously and forever after so many years of employment." I was hurt but I was not ashamed of my work, so I felt that I was unjustifiably being ignored after having presented such a beautiful film.

Mr. Shah and Gouharbai had returned to their verandah where they always sat. I followed not crestfallen, but arrogantly proud and ready to defend myself, striding through the studio while people watched me pass by. After a long silence I could bear it no more so I said, "Should I go to the cashier and collect my dues before I quit, or are you going to fire me from Ranjit Movietone Mr. Shah?" Mr. Shah continued to remain silent and then motioned his peon

Rukma, and ordered him to fetch his Dugla, the Gujrati overcoat he always wore.

Rukma obeyed, and when he handed it to Mr. Shah, Mr. Shah dug into his pocket and signaled to me to get up and approach him. From his pocket he dug up all the money he had, which was a wad of Rs. 2500 and handing it to me, he said in a choking voice, "Kidar I want to put this money at your feet. You have made a sublime movie, this is my humble gift to you." To which Gouharbai added, "You are remarkable, Prithviraj was very impressive, but Monica was superb. This film is rare and only you alone are capable of making such a beautiful and tender film." Our great boss Mr. Shah then said, "I am going to sign Monica to a three year contract, and I will also give her a new chauffeur driven car as a gift. I want you to help sign a contract with her landlord for one year. Ranjit Studio will pay her rent for that period and also pay for a maid servant and a cook to ensure that she is happy and comfortable." Then he rose and hugged me and inquired, "You do like me, don't you?" I was too taken aback by his generosity and kindness, instead of being sacked, which I had expected. He proceeded to tell me that he had decided to increase my salary by Rs. 500 more to Rs. 5500 per month.

Mr. Shah decided to make a film based on the great singer Tansen, and because K. L. Saigal was the Bing Crosby of Indian cinema, only he could fit the role. A contract was signed for the loan of Mr. Saigal for a fixed period, and not on an assignment basis. Mr. Jayantibhai was to direct the film. I was happy to have my old friend around again. When Saigal's work in *Tansen* was over, there were still nine days remaining of the contract period. Miss Gouharbai and Mr. Shah must have considered me a 'genius' or a 'magician' I don't know which, because they asked if I could do a subject which would finish Saigal's work in nine days. I offered them a story called *Bhanwara*, and with their okay, completed the job in time. Incidentally this film also starred Arun, the present star Govinda's father.

During this period a party was thrown in Juhu, which in those days was a remote, deserted area where a few rich people had built bungalows on the seashore, for weekends. Saigal was invited, with the freedom to bring along any one else for company, and he asked me, his friend, philosopher and guide to accompany him. The party was in full swing with drinks flowing freely, and after a couple of hours, Saigal suddenly became restless and asked me to accompany him onto the lonely seashore. He alone had picked up the faint sound of somebody singing raag Bhairavi. We followed the voice and reached a fakir, who was in raptures as he sang Ghalib's "*Nukta cheen hai gham-e-dil...*" Saigal sat at his feet listening with tearful eyes, and putting his hand in his pocket, placed all the money he had at the feet of the fakir. It was on our return, when people inquired about Saigal's absence that this incident was narrated. Then someone said. "You had more than Rs. 5000 in your pocket, did you not count the money?" Saigal's reply was, "He who gives me, you think He counts?" Such was Saigal's nobility.

Snehal Bhatkar, my music director, told me about another incident that happened when he was a musician with

H. M. V. It seems that Saigal was scheduled to record a song at their studio. In those days tape recorders were not yet available and to make a record, the song had first to be recorded on wax. All the musicians had started rehearsing but there was no sign of the singer. When Saigal walked in to record the song, '*Madhukar shyam hamare choor*' he was staggering. Every one thought the take would have to be cancelled, because he looked dead drunk. Standing in front of the microphone while supporting himself with one foot on a chair, Saigal said, "Yes, I am ready, please ignore my stumbling, it is my silly body that misbehaves. I sing, not with my body but with my soul, and the take will be perfect." He sang so beautifully that from the recordist to the musicians, all applauded spontaneously. People did not know that he suffered from sciatica, and alcohol made life bearable.

Health problems forced Saigal to retire earlier than he might have done. He moved to Punjab, his liver ruined by alcohol, and the doctors giving up any hope of curing him. His brother told me that towards the end, his doctor said he might just as well be allowed some alcohol, and left. Saigal hinted to his brother that he would like a sip. His brother concealed the bottle, and pretending to pour, filled the glass with water instead. Saigal took a sip and quoted, "*Bajaye meh diya paani ka ik gilass mujhe, sumajh liya mere saqi nay budhawas mujhe.*" And the great soul passed away. He was a poet to the end.

Chapter 13

Go west young man

For my film *Kaliyan*, I had written *Aab kay naa saawan aaye sakhiree, – jal lay kur humri aankhon say, sautan ghar phool khilaiye*, (Now the season will not return my beloved, take the tears from my eyes to sprinkle the flowers) and Chisti set it to beautiful music. After another two years when I had completed another movie called *Dhana Bhagat* for Ranjit Studio, I was selected to go to the U.K. and U.S.A. as a member of the first Indian Film Delegation. Since the Second World War was still in progress, many prominent people like Mr. Shah and Mr. Mukerjee were afraid, and declined to go. I thought that this was an honour and a rare chance and so I immediately applied for my passport, visa and all the necessary papers. And though I was most anxious to go, once again destiny put me in an awkward position. My beloved son Billy, the youngest in the family was stricken with diphtheria, a deadly disease at that time, and was admitted to the Infectious Diseases Hospital. While I was busy making preparations to go abroad, my child was fighting for his life.

Because he was so seriously sick, my wife had also moved to the hospital, so she could be near him night and day. I was left to care for Vikram and Prabha, my two other children. I was very worried and prayed to my Master, the Almighty for help.

Billy had been released from the Hospital, and although he returned home he was still in a critical condition and required frequent medical attention. So the family physician Doctor Kulkarni visited him daily and treated him with expensive drugs.

One fine day I announced, "I am flying tomorrow early in the morning. We have finally been given clearance." My wife was quite upset and remarked, "You are heartless, you have a very sick child, and you want to go to a foreign land." Billy overheard his mother's remarks and when she went to the kitchen he called me and asked me to sit by him near his bed. Then he whispered, "Please Dad do not miss this golden opportunity of going abroad with this important delegation. I am sorry I cannot see you off now, but I give you my word of honour, that when you return I will be there to greet you with open arms." I was moved by the bravery and strength of this little boy and hugged him.

The year was 1945 and the only way to travel abroad was on a Dakota airplane. Bombay did not have a formal air terminal. Every morning you were asked to report to a hanger and if the weather and safety conditions permitted, only then would the plane take off. Otherwise you had to go home and try your luck the next day. The air journey was very uncomfortable. There were only about sixteen passengers in the plane and we were seated on a bench, as one sits in a railway train. Eight on either side facing each other. Most of the people facing us were Europeans. The plane had to land several times to fill gas, before we were to reach London. We hit many air pockets as we flew over the hot desert, the plane plunging several hundred feet, like an elevator out of control. It was really frightening. The people seated across me were military men and after a couple of harrowing plunges they started vomiting, holding paper bags to their mouths. I refused to get air sick. We were mostly served orange juice, and I got to dislike it so much that for the next twenty years I refused to even have a sip of it.

I remember landing in the desert where we were told that we would have to break for about eighteen hours. I forget the name of this particular town but it was very peculiar, like a place in a fairy tale. The banks, shops and even the post office opened only at night. This place also had several open air theatres, where tourists gathered. It was the first time I saw a beautiful belly dancer. Only her belly moved rhythmically at rapid speed while the rest of her body was perfectly still. She could even make her breasts move to the music at will and in different directions.

We reached London at last in very bad shape, due to the bombing as the war was still on. Being a vegetarian I found it very difficult to find food of my choice in restaurants. People considered fish and eggs to be vegetarian and so I had to forgo my regular three meals a day. A big peach, imported from Spain, cost one pound. I had taken enough money, because at that time there were no restrictions on foreign currency. In fact I carried exchange worth more than Rs. fifty thousand with me at that time.

I preferred to stay at a suburban hotel, about 35 miles from London. It had magnificent oak trees and a very beautiful lawn. Dinner was served punctually at 8 pm. sharp, and if you were not present at your allocated seat at a particular table in the dining room, your dinner was just left there. I was always late for dinner because I used to ride into town to see English movies and return after 9:30 pm. to the hotel by taxi, or bus. The elderly lady who was in-charge of the meals, always waited for me and made sure I got a hot meal. When I approached her to thank her for her extreme kindness and thoughtfulness, she replied, "I do it because you remind me of my son who joined the army to fight for the honor of this country, but last month he died a hero's death. He walked and dressed just like you, with a bow and tie and also had a keen sense of humor just like you. So you see I am not doing a special favor to you, I am just selfish and I am indulging myself pretending he is still alive," and she began to sob. From that day onwards I stopped coming late for dinner.

Another baffling incident happened to me, which I have never been able to understand or explain till today. While I was in London I went to a huge bookstore called Foyles. It was a massive store with several floors where rare collections of all kinds were kept. When you entered you went to the front counter and told them the subject you were interested in and they would then direct you to the proper floor. Since my passion is for poetry, I approached the attendant at the front counter and asked, "On which floor do you sell books on poetry?" He directed me to the top floor and said that when I reached there, the lady in charge would look after me. I remember distinctly that I did not exchange any more words with him, nor did I reveal the title of the book I was interested in. I wasn't even sure if this particular book would be available here. As I reached the top floor. I walked towards an elderly sales woman and said, "Good morning Madam…" She did not let me finish my sentence and said "I know, I know which book you want, son, we have only one copy left with us, please help me with the ladder." I was awestruck and did as I was told. She climbed up the ladder carefully and retrieved a book from the top shelf. Then climbing down she handed it to me. I was amazed. The book was *Lala Rukh*, the very book I had come to buy. I also had heard stories about the curse that went with this book. It was said that anyone who bought this book, would have only one year to live. When I opened the title page, it had the names of scores of people who were its previous owners. I took a pen and added my name at the bottom of the list, since

I was not going to be frightened by rumours and superstitions.I took the book back to my hotel and enjoyed reading it. I decided to go back to the same bookstore to get a copy of the quatrains of *Omar Khayyam*; I have been a collector of his book of poems and do own several editions from various places and countries. When I went back and once again went to the top floor of the bookstore I looked for the lady who had sold me the copy of *Lala Rukh* the day earlier. But I could not see her. Instead there was a man seated there who had seen me the day before and I too recognized him.

He said, "Good morning Sir, here is a note I was asked to hand you, from the lady you met yesterday." And he handed me a piece of paper. I unfolded it and inside was scrawled. 'My job is done, so I return thither, from whence I came.' I was shocked and completely puzzled and so I inquired. "Where is the lady, where has she gone?"

He replied in a sad tone, "She died, last night Sir, She died, suddenly just died after she handed me this paper for you." I still wonder, till today, the complete meaning of this very puzzling event.

In London we were taken to meet many important film makers including Mr. Gabriel Pascal, the great Sir Arthur Rank of Arthur Rank Productions. We were even allowed to watch a shooting of the movie *Caesar and Cleopatra* which was being shot at Pinewood Studio. I was baffled by the set where 'The Hanging Miniature' of the architecture on the River Nile was suspended in midair. I learned more about direction and production from meeting many technicians, actors and directors. It was a real education.

We then proceeded to America to visit Hollywood. Among the other delegates with me, Mr. Sundar Rajan from Madras, and Mr. Hirlekar and Mr. Shorey had already departed for the USA, while Mr. P.N. Roy from Calcutta had decided to return home. My trip to the USA was quite an adventure. I wanted to visit New York first and spend a few days there, before going to Hollywood, California.

Stranded at the airport, because the flights seemed full, I was hoping to plead with the airline staff for a seat. The young lady at the counter was busy on the phone. So I waited. When her conversation was over, she turned to me and remarked, "My boyfriend says my foot. Imagine that!" I retorted, "Madam, that's a fifty percent lie." She laughed most heartily and went out of her way to get me the flight I wanted.

In New York, I had heard of the world famous Waldorf Astoria Hotel, where, in those days I paid $500 per night. My other friends and delegates declined to stay there, saying that it was far too expensive. But I wanted to experience the luxury, and feel like a prince for once, and so decided to stay there. In the hotel lobby was a beautiful, huge statue, about 10 feet tall and a masterpiece in my judgement. It was the statue of a man protecting a woman and child. I was told that it was forbidden to photograph the statue. But I could not resist this wonderful piece of art and I had to capture it on film. So I ingeniously placed my camera in a shoe box, with a small hole in the side which I could uncover with my hand. The lens of the camera was strategically placed behind this hole. I sat in front of the statue and opened the hole exposing the film for at least two minutes, since there was so little light inside. I admired the taste of the people who selected that fabulous piece of art.

At M.G.M. Studio I met Mr. Glassberg, who was the Chief Cinematographer at that time. We seemed to have hit it off very well and he even invited me home to meet his charming wife. I even experimented with cooking an Indian meal in their kitchen. He invited me to watch shooting, but requested that I keep silent during the filming, and only ask questions later in private. I forgot his instructions while I was watching a particular scene. After the shot the actor was powdering his nose and an elderly make-up man was holding up the mirror for him. Suddenly in my shrill voice I asked., "You had a stunt hero who was once a big star, a Mr. Eddie Polo, where is he now?" Mr. Glassberg instead of responding, kicked my foot softly and gestured that I should stay mum. Not understanding his signal I repeated the question with more gusto. The make-up man then turned to me and said, "Sir, I am Eddie Polo. In Hollywood you can be a star today, and tomorrow a make-up man, or a spot boy, or a truck driver. That's show business for you."

All the members were invited to meet the great Cecil B. De Mille in his office. He treated us very graciously and I praised him for his remarkable film *The Ten Commandments*. Soon he started bragging about his achievements, and about his cinematic skill, and how he had shot that spectacular scene of the parting of the Red Sea. He was full of praise for himself and went on and on. I could not resist, and I cut in saying, "But you also rested on Sunday?" He smiled and stopped. He got the message and came over and hugged me. He then asked, "Mr. Sharma, we were told that Indians are only good at snake charming and know very little about literature. But you surprise me. How many people in your industry have the same skill and humour as yourself?" I then proudly told him about the giants like Prithviraj, D.K. Bose, C.J. Shah, and others.

The other thing that impressed me about Hollywood was the attitude of the stars towards their work. I once had an appointment with Mr. Ray Milland who was to report for work in the afternoon for a movie he was making called *The Lost Weekend*. I reached R.K.O. Studio early so that I could wait for him when he got there, but I was astonished to see him already there rehearsing his lines. I was surprised to see him and so went over and greeted him inquiring, "You were to report to shoot only at noon, how come you are already here?" He smiled and said, "Mr. Sharma, once I sign a contract, it becomes a point of honour for me to strive hard and give the best performance that I possibly can." I was quite impressed with his answer because I knew that very few big stars in India had that kind of attitude and dedication towards work. Many of them felt that they are obliging the Producer and Director with their presence.

We were taken around to see how cosmetics are made. Our guide, the public relations officer, went on and on about what all Max Factor had done. Max Factor this, Max Factor that, till our tour ended in the reception, now occupied by a very pretty girl. I merely asked, "Max Factor?" The other quip I recall is telling Doris Day's boyfriend, "Every dog has his day."

The other person I was greatly impressed with was Walt Disney. We became friends and he even gave me a memento, an autographed picture of a frame from his movie *Bambi*. He even said to me, "Mr. Sharma I do not believe in reincarnation but somehow I feel we were once brothers."

I was in New York when the second world war ended, and witnessed the relief, rapture, elation and celebration on that day on the streets. I returned to India having gained a lot of knowledge and experience and true to his word my son Billy received me at the airport. The next day when I reported to Ranjit Studios, I was shocked to learn that Mr. C.J. Shah, the lion hearted boss, had lost Rupees one crore (Ten million) while gambling. He had mortgaged everything to honour this huge debt.

On Mr. Shah's earlier instructions, I had brought back from America a back projection machine, from Paramount Studio with twin projectors, that synchronized the image and made it sharper. Because of the terrible shape Ranjit Studios was in, this equipment was never claimed or cleared from customs. I was even forced to consider, how to produce and direct my own movies.

Shortly after I moved to Bombay, a new tenant arrived in our building. One morning when I responded to the doorbell, the new tenant Mr. Akthar Mirza called on us because his telephone was dead, and he asked if he could use our phone. I said, "Of course you can use the phone, please come in." This chance meeting caused us to meet often, and we soon became very good friends. He had observed my wife's good nature of always offering tea or something to the servants when they came to work. He had also noticed her general behaviour, and had often said, "*Bhabhi*, you are the lady of Ferreira Mansion." Although Akthar Mirza was in the aerated drinks business, he had a very good command of English, Urdu and *Farsi* (Persian). He was very well read with fine literary sensibility, so I asked why he did not attempt writing. He seemed diffident so I told him I had a story ready, and he was welcome to use it. Akthar Mirza went on to become an established film script writer, and was in B.R. Chopra's core group that wrote for films like *Wakt* and many more. Years later, both his sons Aziz Mirza and Saeed Mirza became well known film directors, each in his own style. They are good enough to acknowledge that I was their inspiration.

In November of 1946, Pundit Gyan Shankar, the famous dance director came to my office in Ranjit Studios and said, "Sharmaji, Producer-Director Mazhar Khan has brought my 'daughter' from Lahore. I want you to kindly see her dance once. May be you will find some role for her. They are poor people who need help, and you have helped many new faces and given them stardom. But to go and see her you cannot go in your big car, because Mazhar Khan has ordered the watchman not to allow any producer's car into the premises." Since the distance was short, I agreed to walk with Punditji. When we reached there, I was shocked to see that the family was housed in a large bathroom, with a tub full of water right in the middle of it.

Pt. Gyan Shankar had not informed them when he would bring me, so my visit was quite unexpected. Geeta's mother did not know where to ask me to sit as there were no chairs or stools of any kind. Finally a wooden plank covered with some cloth was laid across the tub full of water, and I was requested to sit on it to watch Geeta's artistry as a dancer. The moment I sat down, there was a giggle from behind the door. That was the first time I heard Geeta. Then she came and danced. It was Geeta's nymph like naughtiness that finally persuaded me to select her for my film *Suhag Raat*. She was not at all beautiful, but she had a certain charm and innocence, a bit of tomboyish flavour. " *What is most beautiful in virile men is something feminine; what is most beautiful in feminine women is something masculine*." – Susan Sontag.

She had hardly had any formal schooling, and was relatively illiterate. On the first day of her visit to my office she asked, "Is the word *Malbat* or *Maltab*?" She was referring to the word Mutlab (meaning). I told her both were o.k. as far as she was concerned. For the outdoor shooting of *Suhag Raat*, the unit had gone to Kolhapur. Geeta was playing the role of a simple girl, tending to her sheep and goats when the animals started drinking water from a drain. Since it was a silent shot, I shouted from behind the camera. "Geeta pretend that you are like your sheep, so we can show you drinking water with your animals." She obeyed and drank half a bucket of the dirty water. She had to be hospitalized, and shooting was suspended for three days.

It was her devotion to work that created a soft corner in my heart. I have already confessed, I am no angel. Yes I was fascinated by this simple, illiterate beauty. As an actress, I am proud of the fact that she learned from me to express a much wider range of emotions than anybody else discovered by me.

For *Suhag Raat*, Bhatkar composed the music of songs like, *Room jhoom mutware baadal chhaa gayae...*, *Choad chalay mu moad chalay...*, *Javo javo na satavo...*, *Mayray dill key dhadkano main sakhi kaun aa sumaiya*. There is a couplet in this song, which became quite significant in my life subsequently, but more about it later.

I must mention Pesi Patel among my experiences. Pesi Patel was a character actor whom I selected for a number of my films. He was a very impressive actor besides being a thorough gentleman, a rarity in film circles. In his younger days he was very fond of motorcycles and used to drive his young wife around. One day there was a mishap and his wife had a miscarriage, following which she died. That night he placed a rose on the bed they shared and he slept on the floor. This he did every night for the next fifty years till he died. I do not know of many love stories more tender than this.

The partition of India was too painful for me to write about. I had no news of my old parents and my three nieces who were living in Narowal. I heard from a family friend that they somehow managed to climb on top of a train going towards Delhi. They were part of the biggest migration of human beings in the history of the world. Many days later they reached Bombay and my mother was weeping because she hadn't eaten for 7 days. They told me that when they vacated our ancestral home my father pulled out his best photograph, and put it on the wall so that the next occupant would know whose house it was. My mother cleaned the house thoroughly so that the next occupant should not think that the previous woman occupying the home was negligent. One starving poet Kaif Irfani, from Rawalpindi wrote: "*Bahaar aati hai laykin kub chaman taqseem hoote hain, bahaar iss shart pur ayee chaman taqseem ho pehlay....kaha uss ne chirag-e-anjuman roshan kiya jaye magar noor-e-chirag-e-anjuman*

Taqseem ho pehlay." (Spring comes but does not divide gardens, this spring demands it as a precondition.... He [Jinnah] asked for the flame of freedom to be lit, but the illumination thereof be divided first).

Roshan had just resigned from All India Radio Delhi and come to Bombay to try his luck. He was in dire need, and I was about to start my film *Neki Aur Badi*, so I told him to start composing the music the very next day. This is the only film in which I attempted to play the male lead. With the release of *Neki Aur Badi*, the bubble of Roshan's hopes burst. The picture was a flop and so was its music. Nobody needed him as a music director.

But somehow, I had faith in him; his knowledge of music and his will to succeed prompted me to try him once more. When I expressed that I would give Roshan another chance every member of my unit ridiculed me for such a suicidal move. But I seldom listen to the opinion of others when it comes to selecting new talent. When I had selected Raj Kapoor as a hero, Madhubala (Mumtaz) or Geeta Bali as a heroine, there was not a single person who had opined in their favour. So I stuck to my decision.

When reasoning failed, my distributors tried to tempt me with cash. I was offered Rs. 25,000/- more per territory if only I dropped Roshan, and replaced him with any other music director (not necessarily with an expensive name). It was my test now; time wanted to measure my strength and my courage of conviction. Poor Roshan! Like a child, he implored me to drop him from the project for my own safety and gain but I stood firm like a rock. I knew that a single success would change all the opinions.

Annoyed by my obstinacy my distributors parted company and my staff pulled long faces for my choice of the 'little man' as the music director. Somehow I could see a 'giant' in the 'little man.' For *Banware Nain* he composed *Teri duniyan main dil lugta nahin;....khayalon main kissi kay;....sunn bairee balam such bool ray ib kya hooga;....kiyun mayray dil main durrd busaya*; and many more. I must specially mention Mujhe such such bataado – kya, because it is not written as a poem. It is sheer lyrical dialogue set to music. After this film Roshan never looked back.

For me writing for and directing the memorable movie *Jogan* was a great experience. A day before the actual shooting of the film, Seth Chandulal Shah and Miss Gouharbai, his partner, had called me into their private room and confided in me that they had signed two top stars, Nargis and Dilip Kumar, for the main roles, and had enough money to run Ranjit Studios for only one month. They knew that Kidar Sharma was the only director who could finish shooting his film in only 30 days, so I was asked to please accept this responsibility and do the job and oblige. I told Mr Shah to give me a room to sleep in, and Rukma the peon to make me a cup of tea as and when required. He agreed. Thus I could shoot during the day and edit at night. Dilip Kumar (his real name was Yousaf) had worked with directors, who were scared of his personality and skill, and did as he desired. Dilip Sahib realized from the start, that Kidar Sharma was totally different from the other directors. On the very first day I told Yousaf Sahib, "Look Mr Yousaf, you are the champion race horse that wins the races, but not all by yourself, you have Kidar Sharma as the jockey who will be holding the reins." Instead of getting annoyed Dilip Kumar showed me great respect. Being fond of Urdu poetry he loved my penmanship and often asked me which lines of a verse expressed a certain scene? And when I told him the suitable lines, he was thrilled and respected me all the more. I am told he has said to many big guns of the industry how lovable, and how talented Kidar is. Nargis also respected me much and the result was that a film like *Jogan* was completed in only twenty nine days.

When Mohammed Rafi came from Lahore to try his luck in the films, he was told to see me at Ranjit Studios, because it was known that Kidar Sharma helped all newcomers to the best of his ability. Mr. Rafi approached me, and I heard him sing. I then referred him to the experts in Ranjit for an audition. Surprisingly they sent him away saying he did not know how to sing a *Ghazal* ! I told Rafi not to be disheartened because he had the potential to be a top class singer. I also promised that he would sing for me when I become an independent producer. In later years he sang many songs for me. In personal life he was a thorough gentleman.

My movie *Shokhiyan*, in the year 1951, was my most expensive black and white film. It cost me more than Rs.1500000. It featured stars like Suraiya and Premnath. I insisted on being authentic about the Portuguese invasion in the south. The invaders had cannons and superior fire power compared to Raja Tamba who has his sword-wielding supporters. Raja Tamba lost the battle. When the film was released, I too, like Raja Tamba had to face total defeat as *Shokhiyan*, was an utter flop all over India.

Anyway victory and defeat are part of the game. When I thought of starting the movie, I decided to hire Suraiya (a big star at that time) as my heroine in *Shokhiyan*. I went to Suraiya's house at Marine Drive. Her Nani received me and was delighted to learn that I wanted Suraiya for my film. She called Suraiya's Maama who looked after her business. He said, "Suraiya is a very expensive star today and her price is Rs. 125,000 and not a rupee less." I looked at him and said, "In that case I shall have to go back disappointed, as my offer for a heroine like Suraiya is Rs.150,000, and a few thousand more for conveyance etc, but not a rupee less," and I got up to go. He was so shocked to hear me say these words, that he begged me to sign her at my price of Rs.150,000, and so I did.

Suraiya, I found had a heart of gold, and she was a courteous, well behaved, and a very intelligent girl. It was wonderful to work with her, because the film being a costume picture of a bygone era, needed numerous changes in detail, and she imposed no fuss or bother at all. One day when I was shooting at Shree Sound Studios, Dev Anand who happened to visit the studio came to see my shooting too. Suraiya saw him from a distance and ran and whispered to me, "Sharmaji please entertain Dev as best as you can, and I promise I shall do any number of films for you free of any charge." – That was Suraiya, the greatest singing star of the forties and fifties.

Another great gesture I experienced was from Lata Mangeshkar, the greatest female playback singer. When she heard the music of my film composed by Jamalsen, the Rajasthani percussionist, whom I made a music director, she said, "I know Suraiya, your heroine, is a good singer, Sharmaji, but I would love to sing for you, even one line will do." And will you believe it a singer of Lata's stature sang with the chorus in the song *Door desh say aaja ray*. I remember the Mangeshkars liked me, and my music very much. Hriday Nath, Lata's brother, used to see my film *Suhag Raat* at least twice a month on my 16 mm print and projector. At such an early age he had a deep appreciation for music. In *Chitralekha* I had used only *Bhairvi*, in *Suhag Raat* only *Pahari*. His sister Asha was the more versatile singer, with a very wide range from classical to disco music. She was also an ardent fan of mine, and when ever we meet she greets me most respectfully. She has a big heart, she makes me feel important and happy.

I got another assignment thanks to Shri C. Ramchander, affectionately called Anna, a very talented music director who was the co-producer of a film they were planning, called *Jhanjhar*. The 'mahurat', the very first shot of a movie in India is considered auspicious and is blessed by a priest. A large audience is also invited. The 'mahurat' was performed by Shri Shanta Ramji the famous director, for whom I have great respect and who also had a mutual respect for me .

But life is never smooth. The heroine chosen for *Jhanjar*, Kamani Kaushal had the role of a spoiled brat, with Om

Prakash playing her doting father. On the first day Kamani the pampered star of Bollywood, failed to act the scene properly. Her role demanded that she play a naughty nymph who is uncouth, but instead she did the scene with sophistication and style, which was not the way it should be done. After about five retakes I was still not getting what I wanted and I said, "Sorry, let's try it again." In a rage Kamani, suddenly walked out and stormed into her make-up room. I felt insulted and since I too was furious, I told the producer, "I think you shall have to find another director who can work with these super stars like Madam Kamani Kaushal. I shall have my cup of coffee and then I will leave with my assistant Lekh Tandon."

Suddenly, Kamani Kaushal's personal peon came running to me and said that Madam had requested to see me in her make-up room. Everyone was surprised that she was being so respectful and not throwing a tantrum. In fact when I entered her make-up room, she got up and said in a soft voice, "Sharmaji kindly hold my hand, and guide and lift me to that height where I might be capable of playing the role of Seeti the naughty brat in the film." The memory of incidents like this will always be indelibly engraved in my mind. I was so moved by her honesty and understood her frustration, which I had misread as arrogance. I then told her, "I think if only we can rehearse the scenes before the actual shooting, I promise the results will be excellent, so please obey me." She looked me straight in the eye and said,

"I shall always obey you Sharmaji." She did start rehearsing, and gave an excellent performance in the movie. We became good friends and she even played a small cameo role in my film *Gunah* and wouldn't even accept a single rupee for her work.

I always had a very great regard for music directors like Khan Sahib Ustad Jandhe Khan, who composed the music for my first film *Chitralekha*. I love music and have admired Shri Naushad Sahib, C. Ramchander and a host of others. But my most favourite music director was Madan Mohan whom I consider one of the most creative. At my office in Shree Sound Studio, one day when I was busy attending to my music rehearsal with Snehal Bhatkar, my younger brother Himmat Rai who had just come in, had seen Madan Mohan standing close to the entrance. He was listening with rapt attention to the notes of the raga *Yaman Kalyan* that was being played on the harmonium. Himmat Rai came in and told me that Rai Bahadur Chunilal's son Madan Mohan was standing outside, and he must be invited in cordially, and personally by me. So I went out and greeting the young budding genius with a smile said, "Please come in, I shall feel bad if you stand outside to appreciate my kind of music." His response stunned me, he recited with folded hands a couplet by a great poet, *"Main luta raha hoon sajdey abhi teri rah guzar main, teri aastan ke qubail abhi mera sur nahein hai"* (I am squandering reverence, on the path that you traverse, because my brow is not yet worthy of your feet.) What a great person Madan Mohan was, and he became an outstanding composer. There is a story, relevant here, about a man who asked God, in what language he should communicate with Him. God replied, "In Music of course."

Another interesting incident happened when I was assigned the job of directing Kishore Sahu's film *Sapana*. Now Mr. Sahu always thought he was a genius, but his financiers had insisted that the job of directing this movie be handed to me, rather then Sahu attempting to handle it himself. I was therefore invited to have a cup of tea with him and he offered me the job. The film was to star him, and Bina Roy, with Hiralal as the villain. I agreed but insisted that I would have my own favourite assistant Lekh Tandon to work on this project. Mr. Sahu agreed. He however insisted that we work on the outline of the story together. So we worked for about three to four hours daily.

Mrs. Sahu, besides being very hospitable, joined us in our discussions. Now Mr. Sahu insisted that to strengthen the main character in the film he should always carry a gun. After having worked for about twenty days on the story together I said, "Look I have a humble suggestion Mr. Sahu. I suggest that the gun must go off with a loud bang at this stage." Mr. Sahu was puzzled and inquired "What purpose will that serve in the movie." I replied, "Perhaps the bang will wake up the audience who by this time would have gone to sleep out of sheer boredom watching this movie, and perhaps then we can also have another flash which says, Thus ends *Sapana*." Mrs. Sahu burst out with laughter and Mr. Sahu was quite taken aback but controlled his emotions. Luckily Mr. Sahu's brother entered and we decided that we should stop these sessions.

Lekh Tandon had been my assistant for many years and in many films. He was one of the most sincere, hardworking assistants. When at last he left me, he directed many movies himself. The one I liked most was *Amrapali*. He really blossomed as a director and made many more T.V. serials than I ever did. It is a tribute to Lekh's character that he still continues to maintain one of the warmest relationships with me. Even to this day he comes to seek my blessings, and I always encourage him, and pray for him.

My work has won me a lot of fans, from the public to professionals and the list includes the first Prime Minister of India, Pandit Jawaharlal Nehru. One day while Shri Nehru was having his breakfast, he was listening to some music on the radio. As it happened one of my songs from *Suhag Raat* was being broadcast at that time. Pandit Nehru was taken aback by a line in the song which went as follows: "*Aankhoon main aankhen daal toohnay mujhko kya pilaiya, jiss taaray pur nazaar peri woh taara lurkharaiya.*" (When our eyes met I was so intoxicated that which ever star I gazed at, that star staggered). Pandit Nehru being a great admirer of Urdu poetry was quite taken by my selection of words. In his opinion, no one had ever written anything better than the great poet Mir about intoxication and eyes, so he was overjoyed that here was a fresh way of expressing ecstasy.

Pundit Nehru was so struck by my poetry that he asked his staff to find out who had penned the film *Suhag Raat* and when he was told it was a person by the name of Kidar Sharma. He said he was keen to meet this man and that if he ever came to Delhi, his staff had to ensure that a meeting was arranged. One day when I landed in Delhi, I was asked by some Government officials to leave my baggage at the airport and they put me in a jeep. They said that they had been instructed to take me to the residence of the Prime Minister.

I obeyed but deep within me I was afraid, because I knew that I sometimes had no control over my tongue, and I thought that perhaps I might have said something derogatory about Pandit Nehru, in the past. I was nervous as we reached his residence. On entering I was instructed to wait in the living room, since Mr. Nehru was busy on the telephone at the moment. This added more anxiety to my fear. I waited for about twenty anxious minutes looking about the room nervously. Then Shri Jawaharlal Nehru entered and I rose to greet him with folded hands wishing him *Namaste*. Panditji said *Namashkar*, but we both kept on standing. Finally he said graciously. "Please, unless you sit down, how can I take my seat." Such was the nobility, and behavior of our top most politician at that time. Then Panditji said with a smile, "Kidar, I want you to do me a favour, will you oblige me?" I replied. "Sir, you have to order, and I have to obey your command!" He was silent for a while, and then said, "I have been wasting Rs. 5,00,000 every year in trying to produce some sensible films for children, but from Bombay to Calcutta the movie mughals have disappointed me with their results. They can't make a good film for children. Now something tells me that you will not let me down. I want you to make a children's film which we can all be proud of."

With my usual sense of humour I said, "Sir, we have so far rarely made any mature films, so making a children's film should be no problem." He smiled and said, "Look, Madame Mary Fields, the authority on children's films in the U.K., is coming to Bombay for a few days at my invitation. She will be staying at the Taj Mahal Hotel, and you must, with her consent, get two to three hours, proper training from her daily. Will you do that?" I said, "Of course Sir, I will go daily at the appointed time, get proper training, make copious notes, thank her every day and try to be a good student." He laughed and said, "I knew Kidar, would be the right choice." He needed my telephone number, so I gave him my home and office numbers. I made it clear to him that I would undertake the creative and production work, but was no good at administration and keeping accounts. So, Mr. Mahinder Nath was to be appointed the secretary, to look after those aspects. Mr. Nehru nodded his consent fully. That day I was thrilled, as I found the Prime Minister of India so gracious, and felt that he had the innocence of a child, and a childish hearty laugh too.

When Mme. Mary Fields arrived in Bombay after about a month, my training began in real earnest. Soon she found me an intelligent pupil and complimented me on my grasp of the special problems connected with making children's films. After about fifteen days, the lady started feeling homesick and told me, "Kidar, you have learned all that I can teach, so I feel it is time for me to go back home." "As it suits you." I replied, adding, "It has been a pleasure to be your pupil and I am honoured to have such a teacher." She could see mischief in my eyes and she replied, "Thank you for the compliment young man." Sensing that she was in a good mood I ventured to ask, "Are you sending any films to the Cannes Film Festival this year?" She smiled and said, "Kidar, winning an award is a habit with us." I shot back, "I may beat you to it and change that habit, just jot that in your diary." She bid me goodbye and we parted on a happy note, but I knew that her feelings were hurt, in particular her ego.

That night, she called Panditji and told him about my challenge. Pandit Nehru was furious and he called me immediately, saying "Are you an oracle, Kidar." I guessed that Madam Mary had called him to complain about my insolence. I said, "Sir with all due respect, do not yell at me till the results are declared. Just wait for only 21 days more when my film *Jaldeep* is shown, I am confident we will win. If not I will let Mme. Fields behead me and you can both applaud, but till then let us wait and see." Panditji was amused at my cock-sureness and said, "O.K. we will wait for 21 days before we pass judgement."

Though I am one who has never cared about awards, I had a very strong intuition. I cannot explain why, but I felt it in my bones, and I knew that I had made a good movie.

After 21 days my prediction came true. *Jaldeep* won the award at the Cannes Film Festival, and more surprisingly the Award was not in the name of the Children's Film Society, the producers of the movie, but it was made out to me, the director. The award was all the more surprising, because *Jaldeep* was shown without any sub-titles in English or French. But since the plot, the actions and situations were so simple to follow, without actual words, they judged the movie as one of the best. Pandit Nehru was delighted to learn that

Jaldeep had achieved and won such an honour, so when I did meet Panditji after the announcement of the award, he asked me to continue working for the Children's Film Society.

For the next subject, I suggested to him that he should be part of it, and that he could inform children about some of the historical facts about India, and about the culture of this wonderful land of ours. He agreed to do as I had suggested and the next movie was entitled *Bachhon Say Batten* (A chat with Children), and his two grandsons, Rajiv (later Prime Minister of India) and Sanjay were included in the cast.

One day I told Panditji, "Sir, I want to make a sketch of yours, since I am a painter too." Again he laughed and said, "Kidar, you are a poet, painter, singer, and director. How do you manage to do so many things?" And I said, "Devotion, Sir, devotion. My involvement gives me the strength, and my devotion to duty, the results." He patted me affectionately. So I made a sketch of Pandit Nehru. My attempt was to portray him the way I really saw him with a childlike smile and an honesty of soul. Thank God I succeeded because it was a big canvas picture, which I had signed. He liked it so much that he had it framed and hung the picture in his study. So I made a copy of the sketch and requested him to autograph the copy for me. The autographed copy still decorates the wall of my office.

One of the films I made for the Children's Film Society was about the great Indian leader Rana Pratap. Because it was a childrens' film the focus was on his favorite mount *Chetak* and that is what the film was called. When Rana Pratap was being chased his horse tried an impossible jump over a ravine, and almost succeeded but was seriously injured. He payed with his own life, in order to save his masters. Prithviraj acted the role of Rana Pratap, and when Chetak lay dying, Prithviraj asked me what dialogue he should whisper in his pet's ear. I told him, "Animals do not understand words, they love touch so please put your cheek on Chetak's cheek as if saying goodbye with affection till the very last." Prithviraj said, "I am not going to do that, since a famous astrologer has predicted my death due to a horse bite." I assured him that if he died of a horse bite, I would burn myself along with him by sitting on his funeral pyre. So being assured Prithviraj agreed and fortunately nothing happened. Years later when Prithviraj lay dying in the hospital I went to see him, and when I was about to take leave of him he signalled to me to stop and he whispered, "Animals do not understand words, put your cheek on mine." I obeyed and bade my best friend a last farewell. He soon passed away.

I made more than a dozen films for the Children's Film Society. The remuneration was naturally small and since I could not financially afford to produce feature films I decided to seek a job. The reader might recall that the heroine of my first big hit was Mehtab. She had also moved to Bombay and acted in a number of films, during which time she met and married Sohrab Modi, the actor-director, who owned Minerva Movietone. Presumably she must have told her husband I was a very talented director, because Mr. Modi asked me to meet him about an assignment. At our first meeting things fell into place, and he offered me a generous, signing amount of Rs. 50,000. But while handing me the cheque he said, "Here is bread for your family for the next three years." I replied, "Then I cannot accept, because that will be breach of a contract. I already have a contract with the Almighty, that He will feed me." So saying I left.

I joined Shaw Brothers of Singapore in 1958 and on the 11th. of January, I reached Singapore. I was so strapped for cash, that I remember writing in my diary that I only had Rs. 36 with me when I reached Singapore. When I met Mr. Run Run Shaw, the first thing I did was discuss the shooting script with him. His Chinese crew and four script men were however too smart for me and they convinced him that I was 'junk' and that I should be quickly dispatched back to India. I was totally dejected and felt very low that night, and alone in my room I whispered to God, "Please look after your pet joker, the clown." The next morning miraculously at 9:40 am. the doorbell rang and when I opened the door, I found the driver of Mr. Run Run Shah standing at my door. He saluted me respectfully and said, "Mr. Shaw has sent his Rolls Royce to take you to his residence."

I thought Mr. Run Run Shaw had decided to send me back to Bombay, so I went down with the driver, without putting on my gray suit, with its matching bow tie. When we reached Mr. Shaw's beautiful residence and the driver was about to open the door of the car, the graceful Mr. Shaw signalled to him to stop, and he himself opened the door of the car and welcomed me. Then he asked me to follow him for a cup of tea with him first. I obeyed and was amazed when he said, "Mr. Sharma, I have not spoken so far, so let me tell you that your script of *Kaki Kuda* (race horse in Mandarin) is very, very good. I hope it will be a nice comedy. Please do not mind what the team of script writers said the other day in my office. They tried to ridicule you, they are much inferior to you as a writers. I am really proud of you and admire your courage in withstanding their mocking remarks, and you just held your head high and stuck to your purpose and argument. I congratulate you."

That day I was very happy, God magnified my joy further with two letters, one from my pet daughter Prabha, and another from my loving wife Raj. Prabha's letter was as if the entire home and warmth had been wrapped up in a piece of paper. What a loving kid she is, she wrote about the home in such detail, that it brought the flavors and colours of the home alive to me.

God is very fond of abrupt endings. There was also a very touching letter from my ex boss, Mr. C.L. Shah, saying, 'Gouharbai considers you her favourite director, and wants me to write to you to find out when our stray sheep is coming home?' I was moved by the affection and regard shown by my former bosses, whom I had served for several years. So I wrote back, 'The goat will be reaching home soon, very soon.' So I started pretending that I had diabetes and must therefore go back home. Mr. Shaw had an appointment fixed with an English doctor, an authority on the subject. My tests revealed nothing unusual, but I pretended to be sick and complained of giddiness. As a result Mr. Shaw told his production manager to send me home and pay all my dues. He was so hurt by my childish behaviour that he said, "I shall never trust an Indian again in my life." So I came back to Bombay, leaving a letter of profound apology for Mr. Run Run Shaw.

Chapter 14

"The woods are lovely, dark and deep. But I have promises to keep,

And miles to go before I sleep, And miles to go before I sleep."

Robert Frost

I thought since Mr. C.J. Shah had called me to Bombay, he must have some subject in mind for me to direct. So I asked him, "Which subject do you want to produce?" He replied that he had signed up Raj Kapoor and Vijayantimala and that the title of the movie was *Jumuna Ke Teer*. So I made a suggestion to him saying that since *Jumuna Ke Teer* gave the impression that this was a purely Hindu subject, perhaps a title like *Akeli Mut Jaiyo* (Don't go alone) would be more romantic and becoming. He liked the title, but the irony was that Mr. Shah, having called me back all the way from Singapore had decided that this film was going to be directed by someone else and not me. When I asked why. He replied, "Kidar Sharma does not sell." I was terribly hurt. I had burnt my bridges at both ends, I could not return to Mr. Run Run

Shaw who had valued my work more than the man I trusted, Mr. Shah. But you can't stand still.

I did not know what to do. The only way to survive was to start my own production with the scanty resources that I had left. So I took my son Ashok (Billy) as the main hero, and since Tanuja's mother, Shobana Samarth, was very keen to have her daughter work under a star-making director like me, I signed her for the main feminine lead. For the backdrop of the movie I selected Udaipur as the main location. My old unit members, like Snehal Bhatkar, Himmat Rai and D.C. Mehta, my faithful standbys who had worked with me in so many movies before, gladly agreed to work with me, but I did not want to be under obligation to anyone. I had a plot of land in Chembur, I sold that plot for a song as they say, and on a shoestring budget I started the movie called '*Hamari Yaad Aayegi*'.

With fine tuned planning and with total involvement, I plunged into my work and things were moving along smoothly and to my satisfaction. But when we were almost finishing, in the last few days of shooting at Shree Sound Studio, where we had built a large set on Stage No. 2, something very unpleasant happened. There was a scene in which Tanuja was supposed to smash her glass bangles, when she learns that her lover, Ashok is dead. This is traditionally done by a Hindu wife, to symbolically express sorrow and renunciation of the world, following the death of her husband. Since Tanuja was educated abroad, she failed to fully understand what this meant, and she was performing this very clumsily. So I helped explain and demonstrated the force with which she should perform this scene. But suddenly, God knows why, Tanuja decided to leave the set, and without my permission stomped off the set. The entire crew was flabbergasted and could not make out what the girl was up to. She got into her car and just drove away.

My son Ashok took me aside and whispered, "Dad, you'd better telephone her mother and apologize, and request her mother to send Tanuja back to complete the scene." I looked at him and said, "Son, Kidar Sharma does not believe in begging. I have never done it in the past and I am not going to start now. This film is as much mine as it is Tanuja's. I have more at stake. If she does not want to complete '*Hamari Yaad Aayegi*' I will burn the entire movie, it is my money and my loss. I have learned to suffer since my boyhood, but I do not beg for favours. Let us wait for another hour or so and if her mother does not bring her back, well then that is the end of my film." I ordered tea and coffee for the staff and overheard one of the actors saying, "Our Sharmaji is a very strong willed director, he makes movies just as he likes them." Shortly afterwards I saw Tanuja's mother bringing her daughter back to the set. She smiled and said, "Kids will be kids, Sharmaji. Please arrange the shot and Tanuja will do as best as she can, and to your entire satisfaction." Thank God the film was completed according to the script.

I had treated Tanuja as my own naughty child. Some years later she said in an interview with surcharged emotion, "I never understood Sharmaji. He was hard as steel but had a heart full of affection and love." She moved me to tears one day when I had incidentally gone to the set of my friend

Roop K. Shori, where Tanuja was working. Seeing me after many years, she requested the director to postpone the shot she was doing, rushed to me and clinging to me like a child whispered, "I am so proud of you Sharmaji, '*Hamari Yaad Aayagi*' has brought me immense luck, fame, and joy."

When '*Hamari Yaad Aayagi*', having cleared the censors, was ready to be released, there were still hurdles to be overcome. We selected the Novelty Cinema as the theatre in which to release the movie. This theatre has a very large capacity, but at the same time it was undergoing major renovations. To buy tickets you had to go through a restaurant at the corner. However prior to the release of the movie, the main theme song *Kabhi Tunhaiyon Main Yoon Hamari Yaad Aayagi* (Sometime in your loneliness you will remember me) had taken off like wild fire thanks to Shri Amin Sayani, the D.J. of the most popular radio show *Binaca Geet Mala* where he had praised the song as a one *Antra* (one verse) and one *Asthai* (the non- repetitive stanzas in a song) number. This song became an immediate hit with the audience at the very first show, specially with the *Burkha*, veil-clad women. As soon as the song started they would thump their feet and clap their hands to the rhythm of the beat. Soon the movie with a no-star cast was running to packed houses.

The recording of this song*Kubhi Tunhaiyon Main* is a story in itself. Lataji, for whom like millions of music lovers I too have great respect, was approached for singing its play back. She agreed and I promised to pay her the same amount that she charged the others. But destiny and Lataji's driver changed all my plans. On the first day, when after rehearsals the recordist and Lataji said, "They were ready for the take", Latajis driver came to me and said, "Mr Sharma a take is only possible when I am paid Rs. 140/- cash. All producers obey me." My ego was hurt and I said I was not like all producers, and Lataji has not even hinted about this new amount. He smiled and said. "Try." At the eleventh hour Lataji cancelled the take and gave me a new date after some days. I paid Rs. 25,000/- cash to the musicians and the recording staff. The second time the same thing happened I refused to bribe the driver and he got my take cancelled again. Lataji wanted me to take another fresh date, but I told her I had only Rs. 50,000/- for the song and all the amount had gone, so when I have enough money I would ask for a date. My music director, Snehal Bhatkar said, "Please Sharmaji, pay the driver Rs.140/- from my account." I told him, "It is not a question of money it is a question of principle and I am a producer, not an obedient servant of anyone...yes anyone..."

This is when I thought of Mubarak Begum. She was called to my office and after she heard the tune said, "Sharmaji I want to have a word in private with you, kindly come to the other room." Bhatkar smiled and winked smelling some problem. But the truth was simple. She said with tears in her eyes, "Sharmaji we are very poor, the melody is great but very difficult, I haven't eaten for two days could you at least order two slices of toast and a cup of tea for me please." I thanked God for getting an opportunity to feed a hungry child. She then gave the most haunting rendering of the song.

I got a message from Mr. V. Shantaram who now headed the Children's Film Society, to meet him. He said. "The Prime Minister Mr. Nehru has phoned me to get *Khuda Hafiz* written and directed by Kidar Sharma. So please write the subject, select the cast, and complete the job. A limited budget allows me to offer you only Rs. 25000."

I started in real earnest and when the first print was ready I informed Mr. Shantaram, asking him to see the print and offer any suggestions or changes. He wanted the preview at his studio, and we commenced at 2 pm. sharp. While the last scene was still being screened, he got up and rushed out of the private projection theatre. I was hurt and I chased him to remind him about small courtesies. He quickened his pace and so did I, till I caught up with him. He turned and said, "Sharmaji, all my life I have made movies and believe them to be fake and entertainment... but today for the first time, when the abandoned child speaks, 'How noble must have been the person who left me under the shade of a tree, me the unwanted child' these lines spoken in childish innocence, brought tears to my eyes. I never wanted anyone to see my tears. Hats off to you Sharmaji, Hats off to you." This recognition has been, for me, the biggest award I have earned, and, ironically years after I retired, I was once again honored by his children with the prestigious 'Shantaram Award' for lifetime achievement.

Mr. Karimbhai Nadiadwala, signed me to remake my old hit movie *Chitralekha*. He told me he had already signed all the other stars who were to play the various principal characters. They were big stars like Meena Kumari to play the title role and Pradeep Kumar was to play the hero. He had also signed Mehmood the comedian and the big superstar Ashok Kumar to play the key role of the Sanaysi Kumargiri. But Ashok Kumar had put a condition on signing, that he would not shave his head, like Gyani had done in the original version, because he had other engagements and was in the midst of making several movies. This was very reasonable, and given the commitment my producer had made, I still intended to get the best performance from these big stars. The film progressed nicely but as always there is a story to tell and one fine day, while we were shooting a very important scene, in which the heroine Chitralekha narrates her sad past to the hero, Meena Kumari just could not enact the memory of the painful past. She seemed to be just mouthing the words, but showed no emotion in her delivery and her expression was flat and contrived. We tried several retakes of the scene but we were not getting anywhere. I then realized that what she needed was some personal incident that would inspire, and bring her into the right frame of mind to play this most delicate scene.

I remembered that, way back in 1942-1943 when she was a child actress in Ranjit, her mother would always bring her to me, but the poor child would be afraid of me at that time, because I was a famous director. Her mother would always come to me and say, "Sharmaji kindly bless my child, by just putting your hand on her head. Because your touch has worked wonders for so many, and she needs your blessing badly." I did recall blessing the little child, and now she was a big star. To inspire her and get her into the mood to enact the scene just before we were to try the fifteenth retake of the shot. I quietly went up to her and whispered in her ear, "Meena, I feel that your loving deceased mother is watching you from a distance, and she wants me to bless you once again to do this important shot so that she can be proud of you." The words that I had whispered seemed to work like magic. Meena Kumari was so surcharged that she performed the delicate scene flawlessly. But she was so overcome with emotions, the memory of her loving mother, and the past that she fainted and almost collapsed on the floor. I rushed to hold her and prevent her from falling and injuring herself. We revived her by splashing some water on her face and when she did regain consciousness she burst into tears and clutching my hand tightly she said, "Sharmaji do you remember how you blessed me when I was a child, thank you again today. I feel blessed."

The movie was released and although some considered it a masterpiece, it did not do too well with the masses. In thirty years the taste of the movie going public had changed from thought provoking movies, to sensually stimulating, flashy entertainment extravaganzas. And I have never been able to supply the masses with these. Nor have I ever been able to satisfy the cravings of the masses with sexually explicit films, because when I started I promised my parents that I would always make such films, where a father would never be ashamed to view a movie in the presence of his own daughter. But in all fairness I must admit that I have always believed that the first *Chitralekha* was better written and the music score was superior.

One day, before a particular scene I suggested a rehearsal, and Mehmood sarcastically asked, "What is a rehearsal Sharmaji?" My reply to him was that it was a *Sadhana*. Ashok Kumar who was sitting beside Mehmood was partly listening to what I was saying. The next day being a holiday there was no shooting but I was sitting in my office completing some personal work. My peon came to me and said, "Sir, Shri Ashok Kumar has come to see you and is standing at the door." I immediately went out and greeting him cordially, requested him to come in, and asked what had brought him here. He said "Do you know what brings me to your door? Your remarks to Mehmood yesterday regarding *Sadhana*. Kindly help me also with *Sadhana* to achieve perfection." I was amazed that such a big star as Ashok Kumar was at heart so humble.

I moved between films and TV. I was requested by the government channel Doordarshan to make films and serials. I made for them *Bheegi Palkhen*. This was so well appreciated that I ended up getting many more assignments. I had also eased the pace at which I wanted to work, "It's sad to grow old, but nice to ripen." – Brigitte Bardot.

I have not written about my films like '*Sehme Huay Sitaray*', '*Pehla Kadam*', '*Bedardi*', '*Thais*', '*Rangeen Raaten*' and many others because this autobiography would become too voluminous. While jotting down my recollections I have written whatever was uppermost in my mind. It does not contain all that was important or all that was interesting, nor is it always in chronological order. But this account is gathered from more than 50 years of living, and almost 30 years of active involvement in films. There are a host of films and T.V. assignments plus much life experience, worthy of being shared because I made films till I was almost ninety. All this must await a second volume – which is yet nascent. I do not pass judgement, I have only tried to tell the story of the events in my life, and the people who have shaped them, and what I have in turn done for this industry. History will write its own version of what I have achieved, but in all honesty, I think I have left an indelible and lasting mark on the Indian Film Industry. I have achieved what I set out to do.

I am, and I shall always will be, a 'Dream Merchant'.

Finally my own favourite quotation. "*I would rather have men ask, after I am dead, why I have no monument than why I have one.*" – Cato, the elder.

And in my own words, *Kubhi tunhaion main yunn hamari yaad aayegi...*

Kidar Sharma directed his latest film in 1993. This book covers some of his experiences up to the sixties. Non- English words have been italicized, with the emphasis on phonetic approximation. The flavour and ingrained culture of one language does not translate readily into another. If some explanation is attempted, it is with the bleak hope of catching something of the essence of the original, and not to annoy the connoisseurs who can relish the original. While quotations have been acknowledged, errors and omissions may please be forgiven. This manuscript had been read and approved, by Kidar Sharma, before he breathed his last on 29th of April 1999.

FEATURE FILMS WRITTEN OR WRITTEN AND DIRECTED OR WRITTEN DIRECTED AND PRODUCED BY KIDAR SHARMA

DEVDAS VIDUPATI
SAPERA
AULAD
CHITRALEKHA
ARMAN
GAURI
KALIYAAN
DHANNA BHAGT
NEELKAMAL
SUHAG RAAT
NEKI AUR BADI
CHHORA CHHORI
JALDEEP
KAKI KUDA
RANGEEN RAATEN
SCOUT CAMP
HAMARI YAAD AYEGI
JHANJAR
FARIYAD
CHITRALEKHA
MAIKHANA
PEHALA KADAM
PAYSE NAIN
SEHME HUE SITARE
ZINDAGI
KROREPATI
ANATH ASHARAM
VISHKANAYA
MUMTAZ MAHAL
BHANWARA
DUNIYA EK SARAI
BHEEGI PALKEIN

For the childrens Film Society he made more than a dozen films. He also made short films for Doordarshan including *Aise Log Bhi Hote Hain*, *Kagaz Ki Nao*, *Ham Honge Kamiyab* etc.